Revisiting Transnational Broadcasting

Presenting a collection of original chapters, this book reassesses the history of the BBC foreign-language services prior to, and during, the Second World War. The communication between the British government and foreign publics by way of mass media constituted a fundamental, if often ignored, aspect of Britain's international relations. From the 1930s onwards, transnational broadcasting – that is, broadcasting across national borders – became a major element in the conduct of Britain's diplomacy, and the BBC was employed by the government to further its diplomatic, strategic, and economic interests in times of rising international tension and conflict.

The contributions to this volume display a series of case studies of BBC transmissions in various European foreign languages directed to occupied, neutral, and enemy countries. This allows for a comprehensive understanding of the different broadcasting strategies adopted by the BBC in the late 1930s and throughout the war, when the Corporation was under the direction of the Ministry of Information and the Political Warfare Executive.

This book was originally published as a special issue of *Media History*.

Nelson Ribeiro is Associate Professor at the Catholic University of Portugal in Lisbon, where he is the Coordinator for Communication Studies. He is a member of the Board at the Research Centre for Communication and Culture, and vice-chair of the Communication History Section at ECREA.

Stephanie Seul is Lecturer in Media History in the Department of Cultural Studies at the University of Bremen, Germany, and a member of the editorial board of *Media History*.

Revisiting Transnational Broadcasting

The BBC's foreign-language services during the Second World War

Edited by
Nelson Ribeiro and Stephanie Seul

LONDON AND NEW YORK

First published 2017
by Routledge
2 Park Square, Milton Park, Abingdon, Oxon, OX14 4RN, UK

and by Routledge
711 Third Avenue, New York, NY 10017, USA

Routledge is an imprint of the Taylor & Francis Group, an informa business

Introduction, Chapters 1–3 and 5–7 © 2017 Taylor & Francis
Chapter 4 © Kay Chadwick

All rights reserved. No part of this book may be reprinted or reproduced
or utilised in any form or by any electronic, mechanical, or other means,
now known or hereafter invented, including photocopying and recording,
or in any information storage or retrieval system, without permission in
writing from the publishers.

Trademark notice: Product or corporate names may be trademarks or
registered trademarks, and are used only for identification and
explanation without intent to infringe.

British Library Cataloguing in Publication Data
A catalogue record for this book is available from the British Library

ISBN 13: 978-1-138-20245-0

Typeset in Myriad
by RefineCatch Limited, Bungay, Suffolk

Publisher's Note
The publisher accepts responsibility for any inconsistencies that may have
arisen during the conversion of this book from journal articles to book chapters,
namely the possible inclusion of journal terminology.

Disclaimer
Every effort has been made to contact copyright holders for their permission to
reprint material in this book. The publishers would be grateful to hear from any
copyright holder who is not here acknowledged and will undertake to rectify
any errors or omissions in future editions of this book.

Contents

Citation Information	vii
Notes on Contributors	ix

Introduction – Revisiting Transnational Broadcasting:
The BBC's foreign-language services during the Second World War   1
Stephanie Seul and Nelson Ribeiro

1. 'Plain, Unvarnished News'? The BBC German Service and Chamberlain's
   propaganda campaign directed at Nazi Germany, 1938–1940   14
   Stephanie Seul

2. BBC Portuguese Service During World War II: Praising Salazar while
   defending the Allies   33
   Nelson Ribeiro

3. Pawns in a Chess Game: The BBC Spanish Service during the Second World War   48
   Gloria García González

4. Our Enemy's Enemy: Selling Britain to occupied France on the BBC
   French Service   62
   Kay Chadwick

5. Repatriated Germans and 'British Spirit': The transfer of public service
   broadcasting to northern post-war Germany (1945–1950)   79
   Hans-Ulrich Wagner

6. The BBC Polish Service during the Second World War   95
   Agnieszka Morriss

7. Broadcasting by the Czechoslovak Exile Government in London, 1939–1945   100
   Erica Harrison

Index   105

Citation Information

The chapters in this book were originally published in *Media History*, volume 21, issue 4 (November 2015). When citing this material, please use the original page numbering for each article, as follows:

Introduction
Revisiting Transnational Broadcasting: The BBC's foreign-language services during the Second World War
Stephanie Seul and Nelson Ribeiro
Media History, volume 21, issue 4 (November 2015), pp. 365–377

Chapter 1
'Plain, Unvarnished News'? The BBC German Service and Chamberlain's propaganda campaign directed at Nazi Germany, 1938–1940
Stephanie Seul
Media History, volume 21, issue 4 (November 2015), pp. 378–396

Chapter 2
BBC Portuguese Service During World War II: Praising Salazar while defending the Allies
Nelson Ribeiro
Media History, volume 21, issue 4 (November 2015), pp. 397–411

Chapter 3
Pawns in a Chess Game: The BBC Spanish Service during the Second World War
Gloria García González
Media History, volume 21, issue 4 (November 2015), pp. 412–425

Chapter 4
Our Enemy's Enemy: Selling Britain to occupied France on the BBC French Service
Kay Chadwick
Media History, volume 21, issue 4 (November 2015), pp. 426–442

CITATION INFORMATION

Chapter 5

Repatriated Germans and 'British Spirit': The transfer of public service broadcasting to northern post-war Germany (1945–1950)
Hans-Ulrich Wagner
Media History, volume 21, issue 4 (November 2015), pp. 443–458

Chapter 6

The BBC Polish Service During the Second World War
Agnieszka Morriss
Media History, volume 21, issue 4 (November 2015), pp. 459–463

Chapter 7

Broadcasting by the Czechoslovak Exile Government in London, 1939–1945
Erica Harrison
Media History, volume 21, issue 4 (November 2015), pp. 464–467

For any permission-related enquiries please visit:
http://www.tandfonline.com/page/help/permissions

Notes on Contributors

Kay Chadwick is Reader in French Historical Studies in the Department of Modern Languages and Cultures, University of Liverpool, Liverpool, UK. Her current research project examines the history of radio and wartime propaganda in France.

Gloria García González is Professor in the Facultad de Comunicación, Universidad Pontificia de Salamanca, Salamanca, Spain.

Erica Harrison is a Doctoral Researcher in the Department of Russian, University of Bristol, Bristol, UK. Her research examines the the Czechoslovak Exile Government during the Second World War and its collaboration with the BBC.

Agnieszka Morriss is Lecturer in the Department of Journalism, City University, London, UK.

Nelson Ribeiro is Associate Professor at the Catholic University of Portugal in Lisbon, where he is the Coordinator for Communication Studies. He is a member of the Board at the Research Centre for Communication and Culture, and vice-chair of the Communication History Section at ECREA.

Stephanie Seul is Lecturer in Media History in the Department of Cultural Studies at the University of Bremen, Germany, and a member of the editorial board of *Media History*.

Hans-Ulrich Wagner is Researcher at the Hans Bredow Institute for Media Research, Hamburg, Germany. His research explores mediated public communication and the history of media in the twentieth century.

REVISITING TRANSNATIONAL BROADCASTING
The BBC's foreign-language services during the Second World War

Stephanie Seul and **Nelson Ribeiro**

This article introduces a collection of original papers and research project reports considering the history of the BBC foreign-language services prior to, and during, the Second World War. The communication between the British government and foreign publics by way of mass media constituted a fundamental, if often ignored, aspect of Britain's international relations. From the 1930s onwards, transnational broadcasting, that is, broadcasting across national borders, became a major element in the conduct of Britain's diplomacy, and the BBC was employed by the government to further its diplomatic, strategic and economic interests in times of rising international tension and conflict. A review of the literature on the BBC's foreign-language broadcasts sets the stage for the presentation of the articles that compose this special issue of Media History.

Although scholars of international relations have long ignored the importance of transborder communication,[1] there can be no doubt that the media have played a significant part in establishing new diplomatic practices. Prior to the First World War, traditional diplomacy was based on secrecy, formalised relations between governments and diplomats, and interpersonal communication between the diplomatic representatives of nation states.[2] The technological inventions of global communication during the late nineteenth and early twentieth centuries—wireless telegraphy, radio, television—greatly expanded the scope of communicating across borders. For instance, the reach of radio broadcasts is almost unlimited by geographical frontiers, and their reception difficult to control. All this makes radio an ideal medium for governments to spread political communication and propaganda.[3] Because of the advances in global communication technology, and because of the increasing interest of the public in foreign politics, governments could no longer afford to limit their diplomatic practices to traditional channels and to ignore public opinion—domestic and foreign—in their decision-making.[4]

Thus, what came to be known, in the wake of the Second World War, as the 'new diplomacy' takes place in the public view through the media.[5] From the Cold War to the recent activities of the terrorist organisation 'Islamic State' and the tensions between Russia and the West, international relations and conflicts are not only subject to mediation on the diplomatic stage, but the political actors involved use the media to gain international support for their policy or to disseminate fear among those whom they consider to be their enemies. It was, in fact, the recognition that the media do play a major role in conquering foreign publics that led Edmund Gullion in the mid-1960s to coin the concept of 'public diplomacy' as 'the cultivation by governments of public opinion in other countries'—a new expression for the old but discredited term 'propaganda'.[6] According to Nancy Snow, public diplomacy 'has been about governments talking to global publics [.], and includes those efforts to inform, influence, and engage those publics in support of national objectives and foreign policies'.[7] And Philip M. Taylor argued: 'This new phrase formally recognised information as an instrument of national power, alongside diplomatic, military and economic power.'[8] In a similar vein, Joseph Nye proposed in 1990 the concept of 'soft power' to explain how countries can exercise a significant international influence not only through their military capacity ('hard power'), but also through the dissemination of their values, culture and ideology. These are spread not exclusively, but to a considerable extent, through the media.[9]

In times of diplomatic crisis, and even more so in times of war, no government can afford to ignore the technological means and the techniques to inform and influence foreign publics in a desired manner. This deliberate use of information for manipulative purposes has long been termed 'propaganda'. In everyday language, 'propaganda' is often regarded a synonym for lies and ideological indoctrination—a connotation that it acquired in the wake of the First World War. However, despite the controversial debates, during the interwar years, on the nature of the concept (see below), between 1939 and 1945 it was widely used in British government circles, in the BBC, and in public discourse to describe Britain's information policy at home and abroad. Recent communication and historical scholarship has tried to free the term from its pejorative connotation.[10] Following Garth S. Jowett and Victoria O'Donnell, propaganda can be defined as 'the deliberate and systematic attempt to shape perceptions, manipulate cognitions, and direct behavior to achieve a response that furthers the desired intent of the propagandist'.[11]

Seventy years after the end of the Second World War, and in an era of globally operating digital media and omnipresent propaganda spread by states and non-state actors, such as terrorist groups, alike, it seems an opportune moment to reconsider the novelty of transnational broadcasting during the 1930s and early 1940s. First, however, let us briefly explain what is meant by the term 'transnational broadcasting'. According to Michael Brüggemann et al., transnational media are explicitly addressed to audiences outside national borders. Four ideal-kinds of transnational media can be distinguished: First, national media with a transnational mission; second, international media, that is, media from more than two nations that co-operate together and address two or more national audiences; third, pan-regional media that address a specific world region; and fourth, global media that are not restricted to a specific world region, but address a broad transnational audience.[12] The BBC foreign-language services analysed here belong to the first category; they are 'national media with a transnational mission' that aim 'to reach an audience outside the national territory with some kind of political mission that is defined by national governments'.[13]

Today it is taken for granted that nation states and political non-state actors make significant investments into reaching foreign audiences via the media. However, in order to develop an understanding of how these 'public diplomacy' strategies are constructed, it is important to look back into the past at a time when the first electronic mass medium, radio, was a novel tool for disseminating messages to foreign publics. Being a medium that could easily cross national borders, radio was already used in the 1920s for transborder broadcasting in foreign languages. The Soviet Union took the lead, and after the inauguration of Radio Moscow in October 1929 it initiated regular transmissions in French, English and German. Other European countries with colonial empires also started transnational radio broadcasts directed at their colonies in the late 1920s (e.g. the Netherlands) and early 1930s (e.g. France, Belgium and Great Britain).[14] However, these transmissions were operated exclusively in national languages and targeted at the white settlers in the overseas territories under colonial rule. This opened the way for the Axis powers, Fascist Italy and Nazi Germany, to assume the lead in foreign-language broadcasting during the interwar period.[15]

Although transnational broadcasting played an important role during the Spanish Civil War (1936–1939)—with Italian and Portuguese stations supporting Franco's uprising against the Republic and Radio Moscow supporting the Madrid government[16]—it was taking centre stage as a weapon of propaganda and counter-propaganda only in the late 1930s and during the Second World War. On the outbreak of war in 1939 the German *Reichs-Rundfunk-Gesellschaft* was already broadcasting from 39 shortwave transmitters, reaching North and South America, Africa, Asia, Australia and Europe. Other transmitters would be added to the network during the war, enabling it to broadcast in 53 different languages by 1943.[17]

The BBC, on the other hand, was a latecomer in the field of foreign-language broadcasting as it took British broadcasters and the government until quite late to overcome hesitations regarding the nature of propaganda. Following the First World War, 'propaganda' had become a word with a pejorative connotation; disseminating propaganda was regarded as something '"un-English", something foreigners did and democracies only resorted to in wartime'.[18] Thus, while other nations had long begun to address foreign audiences outside their national borders, in the late 1930s there was still a running debate inside and outside the BBC 'as to whether propaganda was "a good thing"'.[19]

Hence, although the Corporation had started its Empire Service as early as 1932, it initiated transmissions in foreign languages only in January 1938 with the launch of the Arabic Service. The service was started on the explicit request of the British government and was London's desperate response to Radio Bari, a station set up by the Fascist government in the south of Italy for disseminating anti-British propaganda in North Africa and among the Arab population of Palestine. This propaganda severely threatened British diplomatic and strategic interests in the Middle East.[20] Now the die was cast, and the BBC began to rapidly expand its broadcasting services in foreign languages. In March 1938, news bulletins in Spanish and Portuguese for Latin America followed. They aimed to counter the anti-British propaganda disseminated by German radio stations in South America that threatened to impair Britain's economic and diplomatic interests.[21] During the Munich crisis in September 1938, broadcasts in German, French and Italian were added—the first British broadcasts directed at foreign audiences in Continental Europe.[22] As previously, these broadcasts were inspired by Whitehall's geopolitical concerns; they were a desperate response to the worsening international climate that threated to develop into a wholesale European war.[23]

When war did finally break out in September 1939 the BBC, again on the initiative of Whitehall, greatly expanded its foreign-language services. The introduction of new languages followed by and large the sequence of Germany's occupation of countries across Europe. Alban Webb writes: 'The Second World War was the making of the multilingual "world service" we recognize today. [...] This explosion in foreign-language broadcasting was consequently imprinted with wartime contingencies and exigencies [...].'[24] During the war, the BBC assured that the publics in allied, neutral, enemy and enemy-occupied nations alike could hear the British interpretation of events. By mid-1945, it was broadcasting from 45 high-powered transmitters in 45 languages into almost every corner of the world, totalling an equivalent of 850 hours per week. More than half of the BBC's foreign-language services were directed at countries in Europe.[25]

Today, the BBC World Service, as it was renamed in 1965, is still broadcasting in 30 languages—excluding English—across the globe. However, since the introduction of the first foreign-language services in 1938, a dramatic shift in languages has taken place reflecting the changes in Britain's international relations. Whereas during the Second World War and during the Cold War the focus had been on European audiences, today the majority of the services are aimed at Asian populations.[26] Over the years, the BBC foreign-language services also underwent changes in their name. British transnational broadcasting had begun in December 1932 with the inauguration of the BBC Empire Service, a shortwave service aimed principally at English speakers in the British Empire. With the introduction of foreign-language services on the eve of the Second World War, the BBC Empire Service was renamed into BBC Overseas Service in November 1939. To this was added a separate BBC European Service in 1941—a consequence of the massive expansion of foreign-language broadcasting during the war. These broadcasting services were administratively separate from the BBC Home Service (for British listeners); they were not financed from the domestic licence fee but from a government grant-in-aid coming from the Foreign Office budget, and they were collectively known as the BBC External Services. As mentioned, in May 1965 the BBC External Services were renamed into BBC World Service.[27]

We have seen that the BBC was a latecomer in the field of transnational broadcasting —only in 1938 and on the initiative of the British government had it begun to create a foreign-language service. The choice of each new language during the late 1930s and early 1940s was dictated by political, economic and strategic necessities; the radio transmissions were meant to compensate for the loss of Britain's influence in the world in the diplomatic, economic and military sphere by rallying the sympathy of foreign publics for the British cause. As Philip M. Taylor has put it:

> [F]or Britain [the use of radio propaganda] was symptomatic of a declining power searching for new and alternative means of defending her prestige from constant attack. It was an attempt to preserve credibility not only for Britain but for democracy as a viable alternative to totalitarianism.[28]

As with its domestic transmissions, the BBC adopted in its foreign-language broadcasts a strategy of presenting itself as a credible and objective source of information in opposition to German and Italian broadcasts that were known for frequently presenting lies. Indeed, the BBC's claim to objectivity functioned as 'a propaganda weapon—a demonstration of the superiority of democracy over totalitarianism'.[29] In internal discussions, however, the Foreign Office made no secret that it considered the BBC foreign-language broadcasts the propaganda arm of the state, yet this fact had to be kept secret in the public's eye so as not to jeopardise the credibility of the Corporation. A memorandum of early 1938 stated:

> It was [.] decided that it was important to safeguard the independence of the BBC in the eyes of the public [...]. In point of fact the BBC work in continuous consultation with die Foreign Office [...] as regards the policy on which the foreign language broadcasts are based and as regards the matter broadcast.[30]

Nevertheless, although the Corporation 'was neither independent nor truthful during the war',[31] it became the most important instrument for disseminating news in Europe—in enemy and enemy-occupied territories as much as in the neutral countries under authoritarian rule (such as Spain and Portugal). While listening to foreign radio stations was forbidden under threat of punishment in Germany and in German-occupied territories, a large number of people did take the risk of listening to the British broadcasts. In neutral countries, in contrast, listeners would often gather in private houses and public places to hear the latest news from London. The BBC thus became one of the most important tools used by the Allies to win the minds and hearts of foreign publics during the war, and it was instrumental in creating a transnational communication space for the British interpretation of the conflict.[32] As a result, listening to the BBC's news bulletins—often secretly and under life-threatening circumstances—has in many European nations become an integral ingredient of the historical memory of the Second World War.[33]

Historians have emphasised the importance of the BBC's foreign-language broadcasts in supporting British diplomacy during the 1930s and in reinforcing Britain's war effort against the Axis powers. Asa Briggs' multivolume *History of Broadcasting in the United Kingdom*, originally published between 1961 and 1979, and Gerard Mansell's *Let Truth Be Told* published in 1982, remain important sources for the history and organisation of the BBC Overseas Service as a whole as well as for individual services in particular.[34] Philip M. Taylor has traced the evolution of the BBC's foreign-language services within the framework of Britain's 'cultural diplomacy' during the interwar years.[35] Michael Stenton has highlighted the role of the BBC in Britain's policy of stirring up popular resistance against the German occupation forces in France, Denmark, Poland and Yugoslavia, while David Garnett provides a general account of British political warfare, in which the BBC played a central part.[36] In her unpublished M.A. thesis, Helen Giblin studied the evolution of the BBC's foreign-language services from the perspective of Britain's political priorities.[37] Two recent edited collections of essays offer insights into various aspects of the history of the BBC World Service without, however, dealing specifically with the late 1930s and early 1940s.[38] Other recent studies of the BBC foreign-language services have primarily focused on the Corporation's role during the Cold War.[39]

Nonetheless, there are still surprisingly few historical studies of individual BBC foreign-language services attempting to synthesise the history of transnational broadcasting with British government policy prior to, and during, the Second World War. The best documented service is probably the French Service.[40] Peter Partner's 1988 history of the Arabic Service remains the most comprehensive study of the BBC's oldest foreign-language service, while Niccolò Tognarini and Arturo Marzano have focused on transnational Anglo-Italian propaganda interactions in the Mediterranean during the 1930s.[41] An early study by Jeremy Bennett focused on the role of the Danish Service in supporting the Danish resistance movement, whereas Nelson Ribeiro has recently analysed the BBC broadcasts directed to neutral Portugal.[42] Ioannis Stefanidis has provided a comprehensive account of British propaganda to the Balkans which attempted to compensate for the lack of Britain's diplomatic and military power in that region. His study deals extensively, among other forms of propaganda, with the BBC broadcasts directed to Albania, Bulgaria, Romania, Greece and Yugoslavia.[43] So far no systematic studies are available on the German Service or the service directed to neutral Spain during the Second World War.[44] Similarly, study of the BBC's services directed to Eastern Europe has been very limited.[45] As regards the BBC's Italian broadcasts, we are similarly lacking a thorough analysis of the service as a whole, but Ester LoBiundo has recently published a short book focusing on the year 1943.[46]

This special issue seeks to stimulate further research by revisiting selected BBC foreign-language services directed at European audiences before and during the Second World War. The articles, based on original archival research, are arranged in accordance with their chronological focus. While the focal points and methodological approaches of the case studies vary, they are connected by a number of common interests: First, they investigate the political circumstances under which the individual foreign-language services were introduced and address the sometimes thorny relationship between the BBC and the British government with particular reference to British foreign policy towards the countries in question. Second, the articles raise issues of journalism ethics by exploring the delicate relationship between truth and objectivity on the one hand, and propaganda on the other, in broadcasting under wartime conditions and governmental control. Clearly, Whitehall and the BBC's journalists were pursuing conflicting interests in the sphere of transnational broadcasting: Whereas the government pursued a propaganda strategy in support of its diplomatic interests and strategic necessities, the journalists were committed to the principles of truth and objectivity in selecting news items for broadcasting.[47] Still, the BBC foreign-language services acquired a reputation for accuracy and credibility that holds until this day. Third, the articles consider the BBC's foreign-language services from a transnational perspective: Before and during the war, the BBC was deeply involved in the foreign policy process of the British government, transmitting London's foreign policy and warfare to European publics and thus creating a transnational communication space.

The special issue opens with Stephanie Seul's study of the early years of the BBC German Service during 1938–1940 as an example of British attempts to influence public opinion in (potentially) enemy countries. The article reveals how Prime Minister Neville Chamberlain sought to integrate transnational broadcasting into his appeasement policy and later warfare towards Nazi Germany in a desperate attempt to win over the German public to his foreign policy aim of saving peace in Europe. However, the BBC's employment for official propaganda raised delicate issues of the control of the Corporation by the government and hence of the objectivity and credibility of its broadcasts. The article traces the evolution of a propaganda strategy in which the claims to 'truthfulness' and 'objectivity'—as compared to the lies of Nazi propaganda—became key arguments.

The following two articles shift the focus from broadcasting to an enemy audience to broadcasting to neutral countries. As Nelson Ribeiro and Gloria García González demonstrate, the BBC's Portuguese and Spanish transmissions, inaugurated in June 1939, were considered strategically important by the British government due to the authoritarian nature of the governments in Portugal and Spain and the persistent attempts of German and Italian radio to influence public opinion on the Iberian Peninsula. Ribeiro's article analyses the editorial line of the BBC Portuguese Service and the difficulty of steering a middle course between selling British policy, which demanded from Portugal to end exports of raw materials to Nazi Germany, without offending its authoritarian ruler, Oliveira Salazar. García González, in turn, focuses on the BBC's delicate mission, during 1939–1945, of keeping Spain out of the conflict and possibly inducing Francisco Franco's regime to a favourable stance towards the Allied cause. This, however, led to severe tensions between Britain's ambassador in Spain, Sir Samuel Hoare, and the BBC.

In contrast, Kay Chadwick explores the British broadcasting strategy towards the French audience living under German occupation. More specifically, she focuses on representations of Britain to occupied France in the programme 'The French speak to the French.' After examining the establishment of the BBC French Service and the formulation of a British propaganda strategy, Chadwick investigates the efforts of the service to explain and justify British war policy and to foster the belief of the French population in Britain as a reliable friend and ally after the German occupation of Paris in June 1940.

Hans-Ulrich Wagner's contribution takes us back to Germany, offering yet another perspective on the transnational dimension of the BBC's broadcasting services. His article directs the attention from British broadcasting to an enemy country in wartime to the transfer of the BBC's broadcasting philosophy—and of part of its wartime personnel —to the newly established broadcasting system in Northern Germany in the immediate post-war years. The BBC and the ideals of British public service broadcasting thus became a role model and laid the ground for the new broadcasting system in the British occupation zone. Repatriated Germans, who had worked for the BBC German Service during their exile in London, came to play a crucial role as representatives of a new generation of German journalists with a democratic political outlook. They heralded the idea of public service broadcasting, but were often exposed to pressure from conservative forces in West Germany.

Finally, in the research project reports section, doctoral students Agnieszka Morriss and Erica Harrison present their ongoing research on the BBC's role in broadcasting to Poland and Czechoslovakia during the Second World War. As regards the latter, the study focuses specifically on the broadcasts of the Czechoslovak government-in-exile transmitted by the BBC. The research project reports take us back to the issue of how to address an audience living under German occupational rule while fulfilling the demands of Britain's policy towards an increasingly close Soviet ally, whose own political and strategic ambitions ran counter to Poland's and Czechoslovakia's national interests. Both BBC services have hardly been studied; the Ph.D. projects will therefore contribute significantly to our knowledge of British foreign-language broadcasting to Central and Eastern Europe during the Second World War and the dawning Cold War.

This collection of articles and research project reports can by no means cover the whole range of BBC foreign-language services during the Second World War, or all the diverse aspects of British transnational broadcasting and its legacy. Even so, the editors hope that, taken together, the papers will provide an encouragement to further research in this field.

Acknowledgements

Earlier versions of the articles by Hans-Ulrich Wagner, Nelson Ribeiro and Stephanie Seul were originally presented in a panel to the ECREA 4th European Communication Conference held in Istanbul in October 2012. The editors wish to thank the authors who have contributed to this special issue, as well as the anonymous reviewers for their helpful comments, and Tom O'Malley and Stephanie Jones for their unfailing support.

Disclosure statement

No potential conflict of interest was reported by the authors.

Notes

1. Rawnsley, *Radio Diplomacy*, 1.
2. Frankel, *International Relations*, 123–5; Gilboa, "Diplomacy in the Media Age," 1; Snow, "Rethinking Public Diplomacy," 6; Rawnsley, *Radio Diplomacy*, 6.
3. Thussu, "Information Economy," 536; Fickers, "Radio," 870; Fickers, "Broadcasting," 106.
4. Rawnsley, *Radio Diplomacy*, 6.
5. Gilboa, "Diplomacy in the Media Age," 1–2.
6. Taylor, "Strategic Communications," 6; Cull, "Public Diplomacy," 19. The quotation is taken from an early brochure of the Murray Center of Public Diplomacy, quoted in Cull, "Public Diplomacy," 19. See also Webb, *London Calling*, 2–3.
7. Snow, "Rethinking Public Diplomacy," 6.
8. Taylor, "Strategic Communications," 6.
9. Nye, "Soft Power,"
10. Taylor, "Strategic Communications"; Bussemer, *Propaganda*; Jowett and O'Donnell, *Propaganda and Persuasion*; Welch, *Propaganda*.
11. Jowett and O'Donnell, *Propaganda and Persuasion*, 7.
12. Brüggemann and Schulz-Forberg, "Becoming Pan-European?," 698–700; Brüggemann et al., "Transnationale Öffentlichkeit in Europa," 396–7.
13. Brüggemann and Schulz-Forberg, "Becoming Pan-European?," 699. On the transnational character of broadcasting see also Fickers, "Broadcasting"; Fickers, "Radio."
14. On broadcasting to the British Empire see Potter, *Broadcasting Empire*. See also the reviews and comments by Hajkowski et al., "Roundtable."
15. Walker, *Skyful of Freedom*, 26–9; Wasburn, *Broadcasting Propaganda*; Rawnsley, *Radio Diplomacy*, 7–8.
16. Ribeiro, "Using a New Medium."
17. Bergmeier and Rainer, *Inside Story*.
18. Taylor, *British Propaganda*, 91.
19. Briggs, *War of Words*, 81.

20. Partner, *Arab Voices*; Taylor, *Projection*; Briggs, *Golden Age*; Marzano, "Guerra delle onde." See also Webb, *London Calling*, 1–2; Clark, "The B.B.C.'s External Services," 173.

21. Whitton and Herz, "Radio in International Politics"; Taylor, *Projection of Britain*; Webb, *London Calling*, 1–2.According to Clark, "The B.B.C.'s External Services," 173, the broadcasts for Latin America also served the purpose of cloaking the BBC's propaganda activities in Palestine.

22. For detailed accounts of the step-by-step introduction of new foreign-language services by the BBC see Taylor, *Projection of Britain*; Briggs, *Golden Age* and *War of Words*; Seul, "Appeasement und Propaganda."

23. For the circumstances that led to the introduction of German, French and Italian broadcasts by the BBC during the Munich crisis in September 1938 see Stephanie Seul's article in this special issue.

24. Webb, *London Calling*, 13.

25. Mansell, *Let Truth Be Told*, 104, 123; Webb, *London Calling*, 2, 15; Footitt and Tobia, *WarTalk*, 69; Clark, "The B.B.C.'s External Services," 173.

26. Information retrieved from the BBC World Service's homepage, http://www.bbc.co.uk/ws/ languages [last visit: September 18, 2015].

27. Walker, *Skyful of Freedom*, 24, 31, 60, 77–8; Browne, "Going International"; Clark, "The B.B.C.'s External Services," 175.

28. Taylor, *Projection of Britain*, 215.

29. Curran and Seaton, *Power Without Responsibility*, 166.

30. *Foreign Language Broadcasting*, undated Foreign Office memorandum, The National Archives, Kew, London, FO 395/564, P 1263/5/150.

31. Nicholas, *Echo of War*, 8.

32. Badenoch, Fickers and Henrich-Franke, "Airy Curtains," 14 have stressed the 'important role of broadcasting as a central actor in creating a transnational and European communication space'.

33. Lo Biundo, *London Calling Italy*, 9; Seul, "Appeasement und Propaganda," 1356–9.

34. Briggs, *Golden Age*; Briggs, *War of Words*; Mansell, *Let Truth Be Told*.

35. Taylor, *Projection of Britain*; Taylor, *British Propaganda*.

36. Stenton, *Radio London*; Garnett, *Secret History of PWE*.

37. Giblin, "BBC External Services."

38. Gillespie and Webb, *Diasporas and Diplomacy*; Gillespie, Webb and Baumann, *BBC World Service*.

39. Webb, "Auntie Goes to War Again"; Webb, *London Calling*; Rawnsley, *Radio Diplomacy*. For a more general study on cold-war broadcasting see also Badenoch, Fickers and Henrich-Franke, "Airy Curtains."

40. See the literature review in Kay Chadwick's contribution to this special issue. Another recent study is Launchbury, *Music, Poetry, Propaganda*.

41. Partner, *Arab Voices*; Tognarini, "Race for the Arabian Audience"; Marzano, "Guerra delle onde."

42. Bennett, *British Broadcasting and the Danish Resistance Movement*; Ribeiro, *BBC Broadcasts to Portugal*.

43. Stefanidis, *Substitute for Power*.

44. The focus of Seul, "Appeasement und Propaganda" is on the period 1938–1940, while Brinson and Dove, *'Stimme der Wahrheit'* present essays on various aspects of the history

of the BBC German Service during 1938–1999. An early study by Wittek, *Der britische Ätherkrieg* does not make use of official government documents and is largely outdated. For a review of the research literature on the BBC Spanish Service see Gloria García González' article in this special issue.

45. See the literature reviews in the research project reports of Agnieszka Morriss and Erica Harrison in this special issue.

46. Lo Biundo, *London Calling Italy*. The volume contains a brief review of the literature.

47. On journalism ethics see Ward, "Journalism Ethics"; Kaplan, "Origins of Objectivity."

Bibliography

Badenoch, Alexander, Andreas Fickers, and Christian Henrich-Franke. "Airy Curtains in the European Ether: Introduction." In *Airy Curtains in the European Ether: Broadcasting and the Cold War*, edited by Alexander Badenoch, Andreas Fickers, and Christian Henrich-Franke, 9–28. Baden-Baden: Nomos Verlagsgesellschaft, 2013.

Bennett, Jeremy. *British Broadcasting and the Danish Resistance Movement, 1940–1945: A Study of the Wartime Broadcasts of the B.B.C. Danish Service.* Cambridge: Cambridge University Press, 1966.

Bergmeier, Horst J. P., and Rainer E. Lotz. *The Inside Story of Nazi Radio Broadcasting and Propaganda Swing.* New Haven, CT: Yale University Press, 1997.

Briggs, Asa. *Golden Age of Wireless. Vol. 2 of The History of Broadcasting in the United Kingdom.* Oxford: Oxford University Press, 1965.

Briggs, Asa. *The War of Words. Vol. 3 of The History of Broadcasting in the United Kingdom.* Oxford: Oxford University Press, 1970.

Brinson, Charmian, and Richard Dove, eds. *'Stimme der Wahrheit': German-Language Broadcasting by the BBC.* Amsterdam: Rodopi, 2003.

Browne, Donald R. "Going International: How the BBC Began Foreign Language Broadcasting." *Journalism & Mass Communication Quarterly* 60, no. 3 (1983): 423–430.

Brüggemann, Michael, Andreas Hepp, Katharina Kleinen-von Königslöw, and Hartmut Wessler. "Transnationale Öffentlichkeit in Europa: Forschungsstand und Perspektiven [Transnational Public Sphere in Europe: State of Research and Perspectives]." *Publizistik* 54, no. 3 (2009): 391–414.

Brüggemann, Michael, and Hagen Schulz-Forberg. "Becoming Pan-European? Transnational Media and the European Public Sphere." *The International Communication Gazette* 71, no. 8 (2009): 693–712.

Bussemer, Thymian. *Propaganda: Konzepte und Theorien* [Propaganda: Concepts and Theories]. With a foreword by Peter Glotz. 2nd ed. Wiesbaden: VS Verlag für Sozialwissenschaften, 2008.

Clark, Beresford. "The B.B.C.'s External Services." *International Affairs (Royal Institute of International Affairs 1944-)* 35, no. 2 (1959): 170–180.

Cull, Nicholas J. "Public Diplomacy before Gullion: The Evolution of a Phrase." In *Routledge Handbook of Public Diplomacy*, edited by Nancy Snow and Philip M. Taylor, 19–23. New York: Routledge, 2009.

Curran, James, and Jean Seaton. *Power without Responsibility: The Press and Broadcasting in Britain.* London: Methuen, 1985.

Fickers, Andreas. "Broadcasting." In *The Palgrave Dictionary of Transnational History*, edited by Akira Iriye and Pierre-Yves Saunier, 106–108. New York: Palgrave, 2009.

Fickers, Andreas. "Radio." In *The Palgrave Dictionary of Transnational History*, edited by Akira Iriye and Pierre-Yves Saunier, 870–873. New York: Palgrave, 2009.

Footitt, Hilary, and Simona Tobia. *WarTalk: Foreign Languages and the British War Effort in Europe, 1940–47.* Basingstoke: Palgrave Macmillan, 2013.

Frankel, Joseph. *International Relations in a Changing World.* Oxford: Oxford University Press, 1979.

Garnett, David. *The Secret History of PWE: The Political Warfare Executive 1939–1945.* With an Introduction and Notes by Andrew Roberts. London: St Ermin's Press, 2002 [originally written 1945–47].

Giblin, Helen L. "The BBC External Services: National Priorities and the Development of Language Services 1932–1946." MA diss., University of Houston, 1994.

Gilboa, Eytan. "Diplomacy in the Media Age: Three Models of Uses and Effects." *Diplomacy & Statecraft* 12, no. 2 (2001): 1–28.

Gillespie, Marie, and Alban Webb, eds. *Diasporas and Diplomacy: Cosmopolitan contact zones at the BBC World Service (1932–2012).* London: Routledge, 2013.

Gillespie, Marie, Alban Webb, and Gerd Baumann, eds. *The BBC World Service, 1932–2007: Cultural Exchange and Public Diplomacy.* Special issue of *The Historical Journal of Film, Radio and Television* 28, vol. 4 (2008).

Hajkowski, Thomas, Dwayne Winseck, Peter Putnis, and Simon J. Potter. "Roundtable." *Media History* 20, no. 3 (2014): 322–326.

Jowett, Garth S., and Victoria O'Donnell. *Propaganda and Persuasion.* 5th ed. Los Angeles, CA: Sage, 2012.

Kaplan, Richard. "The Origins of Objectivity in American Journalism." In *The Routledge Companion to News and Journalism*, edited by Stuart Allen, 25–37. New York: Routledge, 2010.

Launchbury, Claire. *Music, Poetry, Propaganda: Constructing French Cultural Soundscapes at the BBC during the Second World War.* Oxford: Peter Lang, 2012.

Lo Biundo, Ester. *London Calling Italy: La propaganda di Radio Londra nel 1943* [London Calling Italy: The Propaganda of Radio London during 1943]. Milan: Edizioni Unicopli, 2014.

Mansell, Gerard. *Let Truth Be Told: 50 Years of BBC External Broadcasting.* London: Weidenfeld and Nicolson, 1982.

Marzano, Arturo. "La 'guerra delle onde': La risposta inglese e francese a Radio Bari (1938–1939)." [The 'War of the Airwaves': English and French Responses to Radio Bari (1938–1939)] *Contemporanea: rivista di storia dell'800 e del'900* 15, no. 1 (2012): 2–24.

Nicholas, Siân. *The Echo of War: Home Front Propaganda and the Wartime BBC, 1939–45.* Manchester: Manchester University Press, 1996.

Nye, Joseph S. "Soft Power." *Foreign Policy* 80 (1990): 153–171.

Partner, Peter. *Arab Voices: The BBC Arabic Service 1938–1988.* London: British Broadcasting Corporation, 1998.

Potter, Simon J. *Broadcasting Empire: The BBC and the British World, 1922–1970*. Oxford: Oxford University Press, 2012.

Rawnsley, Gary D. *Radio Diplomacy and Propaganda: The BBC and VOA in International Politics*. Basingstoke: Macmillan Press, 1996.

Ribeiro, Nelson. *BBC Broadcasts to Portugal in World War II: How Radio Was Used as a Weapon of War*. Lewiston: Edwin Mellen Press, 2011.

Ribeiro, Nelson. "Using a New Medium for Propaganda: The Role of Transborder Broadcasts during the Spanish Civil War." *Media, War & Conflict* 7, no. 1 (2014): 37–50.

Seul, Stephanie. "Appeasement und Propaganda 1938–1940: Chamberlains Außenpolitik zwischen NS-Regierung und deutschem Volk" [Appeasement and Propaganda, 1938–1940: Chamberlain's Foreign Policy in Relation to the National Socialist Government and the German People]. PhD diss., European University Institute, 2005. http://cadmus.eui.eu/handle/1814/5977.

Snow, Nancy. "Rethinking Public Diplomacy." In *Routledge Handbook of Public Diplomacy*, edited by Nancy Snow and Philip M. Taylor, 3–11. New York: Routledge, 2009.

Stefanidis, Ioannis. *Substitute for Power: Wartime British Propaganda to the Balkans*. Farnham: Ashgate, 2012.

Stenton, Michael. *Radio London and Resistance in Occupied Europe: British Political Warfare 1939–1943*. Oxford: Oxford University Press, 2000.

Taylor, Philip M. *The Projection of Britain: British Overseas Publicity and Propaganda, 1919–1939*. Cambridge: Cambridge University Press, 1981.

Taylor, Philip M. *British Propaganda in the 20th Century: Selling Democracy*. Edinburgh: Edinburgh University Press, 1999.

Taylor, Philip M. "Strategic Communications and the Relationship between Governmental 'Information' Activities in the Post 9/11 World." *Journal of Information Warfare* 5, no. 3 (2006): 1–25.

Thussu, Daya. "Information Economy." In *The Palgrave Dictionary of Transnational History*, edited by Akira Iriye and Pierre-Yves Saunier, 535–541. New York: Palgrave, 2009.

Tognarini, Niccolò. "The Race for the Arabian Audience. Italian and British Propaganda in the Mediterranean in 1930s: A Trans-National Perspective." PhD diss., European University Institute, 2009.

Walker, Andrew. *A Skyful of Freedom: 60 Years of the BBC World Service*. London: Broadside Books Limited, 1992.

Ward, Stephen A. "Journalism Ethics." In *The Handbook of Journalism Studies*, edited by Karin Wahl-Jorgensen and Thomas Hanitzsch, 295–309. New York: Routledge, 2009.

Wasburn, Philo C. *Broadcasting Propaganda: International Radio Broadcasting and the Construction of Political Reality*. Westport: Praeger, 1992.

Webb, Alban. "Auntie Goes to War Again: The BBC External Services, the Foreign Office and the Cold War." *Media History* 12, no. 2 (2006): 117–132.

Webb, Alban. *London Calling: Britain, the BBC World Service and the Cold War*. London: Bloomsbury, 2014.

Welch, David. *Propaganda: Power and Persuasion*. London: The British Library, 2013.

Whitton, John B., and John H. Herz. "Radio in International Politics." In *Propaganda by Short Wave*, edited by Harwood L. Childs and John B. Whitton, 3–48. Princeton, NJ: Princeton University Press, 1942.

Wittek, Bernhard. *Der britische Ätherkrieg gegen das Dritte Reich: Die deutschsprachigen Kriegssendungen der British Broadcasting Corporation* [Britain's Radio War against the Third Reich: The German-language War Broadcasts of the British Broadcasting Corporation]. Münster: C.J. Fahle, 1962.

'PLAIN, UNVARNISHED NEWS'?
The BBC German Service and Chamberlain's propaganda campaign directed at Nazi Germany, 1938–1940

Stephanie Seul

Established during the Sudeten crisis in September 1938, the BBC German Service played an important role in Chamberlain's appeasement policy and warfare towards Nazi Germany. Yet the BBC's employment for official propaganda, especially in peacetime, raised delicate issues of its independence from government control and of the objectivity and credibility of its broadcasts. This paper discusses, first, the origins of the BBC German Service and its role within Chamberlain's policy. Second, it analyses the relationship between the BBC and Whitehall. Third, it traces the evolution and development of the British propaganda strategy towards Germany and investigates how the concepts of 'truthfulness' and 'objectivity' were internally understood and employed by the BBC and Whitehall in their propaganda campaign. Finally, the paper argues that Chamberlain's propaganda strategy towards Germany collapsed during the Allied campaign in Norway in April 1940 precisely because it no longer conformed to its self-proclaimed principles of 'truth' and 'objectivity'. As a result, the credibility of the BBC German Service suffered a significant, if ultimately temporary, setback.

Introduction

In December 1938 the BBC's magazine *The Listener* stated that the German and other foreign-language news bulletins, introduced during the recent international crisis, aimed to furnish 'plain, unvarnished news rather than [...] sensationalism or propaganda. What matters most', the article asserted, 'is to create among listeners abroad confidence in the truth and authenticity of the British bulletins'.[1] The British press echoed this image. The *Manchester Guardian* declared that the BBC's German-language broadcasts sought 'to transmit the plain truth'[2]; *The Times* argued that they were offering '"straight" news covering important statements and speeches and events of the day at home and overseas [and] that purely propagandistic statements should be excluded'.[3] Likewise, the British Government praised the BBC German Service as an objective news service: 'His Majesty's Government are in entire agreement with the policy adopted by the British Broadcasting Corporation of rigidly excluding propaganda from their foreign language broadcasts',[4] Rex Leeper from the Foreign Office News Department replied to an enquiry from a member of the public.[5]

'Truth' and 'objectivity', on the one hand, and 'propaganda', on the other hand, are commonly viewed as antagonist concepts. In the wake of the First World War, and with the rise of the totalitarian dictatorships in Europe, the term 'propaganda'—which originally meant the spreading of ideas and promotion of opinions—acquired a negative connotation and became a synonym for disseminating lies and manipulating public opinion.[6] Nevertheless, during the 1930 and 1940s, the British Government widely used the term 'propaganda' to denote its own information policy at home and abroad, arguing that its own propaganda was 'good' because it was based on objective information, whereas totalitarian propaganda was deplorable since it contained lies and defamation. Still, this did not exclude the omission of unwelcome facts and the subtle twisting of truths if it suited the purposes of the British Government.[7]

From 1938 onwards, the BBC became the most important medium for the British Government to address foreign audiences and disseminate propaganda abroad. At Whitehall's request, the first foreign-language services were established in Arabic, Spanish and Portuguese for South America, German, French and Italian. Beyond providing 'objective' news to foreign audiences, their purpose was to counter Fascist propaganda.[8] During the Second World War, the greatly expanded BBC foreign-language services were placed under the guidance of the Ministry of Information and the Political Warfare Executive.[9]

How did the BBC perceive its role as a medium of Whitehall's transnational propaganda campaign? From its foundation in 1922, the Corporation had advocated the journalistic principles of truth and objectivity in reporting and of independence from governmental control.[10] However, the historical record reveals that these principles were more an aspiration than a reflection of reality, something that had constantly to be negotiated with, and defended against the British Government. Sir John Reith, the BBC's first Director-General, was convinced that the Corporation must serve the interests of the nation. Hence, although the BBC was nominally independent from the government, over the years a close cooperation—or rather an 'uneasy compromise'—evolved.[11] The first test case for the BBC's relationship with the government was the General Strike of 1926, during which the BBC became the mouthpiece of the government and 'learnt how to censor itself [...] in order to forestall government intervention'.[12]

With the rise of the totalitarian dictatorships the government's pressure on the BBC increased. While the BBC sought to keep up its editorial principles, Whitehall was concerned not to provoke Europe's dictators. Since the BBC was perceived abroad as the official voice of Britain, any criticism of the dictators on the BBC would have been interpreted as reflecting British policy.[13] The government therefore justified its intervention in the BBC's broadcasting on foreign affairs with the 'national interest'. At the same time, it urged the Corporation not to mention such intervention in public.[14] Accordingly, the BBC frequently passed off demands and pressure from Whitehall as its own policy in order to evade official regulations and restrictions from being imposed.[15] However, the relationship between the BBC and the government was not antagonistic. Rather, as Scannell and Cardiff put it, 'The continuous routine contact that had built up over the years between senior personnel in Broadcasting House, Whitehall and Westminster meant that they all abided by the same rules and codes of conduct'.[16]

Although Whitehall closely supervised the BBC's broadcasting on foreign affairs—and in particular the output of its foreign-language services—the BBC claimed in public that 'truth' and 'objectivity' were its guiding principles. Curran and Seaton have argued that these principles became themselves a propaganda weapon that served to distinguish British propaganda from that of the totalitarian dictatorships and to demonstrate the superiority of democracy over totalitarianism.[17] Similarly, Ribeiro maintains that the idea of 'objectivity' in the BBC' Portuguese broadcasts during the Second World War served to boost the credibility and to increase the audience of this news service while at the same time exposing the lies of the German radio broadcasts in Portuguese.[18]

This paper pursues four aims. Focusing on the premiership of Neville Chamberlain (May 1937 to May 1940), it recounts, first, the origins of the BBC German Service and its role within British foreign policy and warfare towards Nazi Germany. Second, it analyses the relationship between the BBC and Whitehall and shows how broadcasting content was tailored to fit the needs of Chamberlain's policy. Third, it traces the evolution of a propaganda strategy in which the claims to 'truthfulness' and 'objectivity' served to enhance the credibility of the British broadcasts in the ears of the German listeners and to propagate the image of a government-independent news service acting as an antidote to the lies of Nazi propaganda. Finally, it argues that Chamberlain's propaganda strategy collapsed during the Allied campaign in Norway in the spring of 1940 precisely because it was no longer commensurate with its self-proclaimed principles of 'truth' and 'objectivity'. As a result, the credibility of the BBC's broadcasts to Germany suffered.

The Role of the BBC German Service in Chamberlain's Appeasement Policy and Warfare towards Nazi Germany 1938–1940

British foreign policy towards Nazi Germany is known as 'appeasement', a doctrine closely connected with Prime Minister Chamberlain who sought to pacify Hitler by granting him substantial concessions. These culminated in the transfer of the Sudetenland to Germany at the Munich Conference on September 29, 1938.[19] At the height of the Sudeten crisis, when Hitler threatened to invade Czechoslovakia and plunge Europe into war, Chamberlain decided to address personally the German people. On the evening of September 27, 1938, the British Government asked the BBC to translate into German and broadcast on all available transmitters a speech the Prime Minister was about to make over the radio to the British nation and Empire. In his speech Chamberlain appealed to all peoples, including the German, to help him save the peace in Europe.[20] From this day onwards, the BBC, at the request of the British Government, regularly broadcast a German-language programme of news and political commentaries.

To direct propaganda in peacetime at a foreign public over the heads of its government was a very new concept that evolved during the 1930s in response to the danger posed by the totalitarian dictatorships.[21] However, it was a hazardous undertaking, for it threatened to worsen relations with Europe's dictators. The Nazis' complaints about the alleged anti-German tone of the British media were notorious and accompanied Chamberlain's appeasement efforts since the autumn of 1937. As a result, Whitehall imposed a system of informal political control over the British press and the BBC to prevent critical comments on Nazi Germany to appear in the media.[22] As Scannell and Cardiff pointed out, 'The policy of appeasement [...] began with discreet surveillance of, and diplomatic pressure upon the British media'.[23] Only three months before the start of the BBC German Service there had still been stubborn resistance within Whitehall against widening British propaganda activities for fear of alienating Nazi Germany.[24] Given the risks involved in broadcasting into a media-conscious totalitarian dictatorship, what then motivated Chamberlain to start broadcasting to the German people at the height of a diplomatic crisis?

Chamberlain's principal reason was the realisation that Britain and France were militarily unprepared for war against Germany.[25] Propaganda offered a small chance to avert war by winning over the German public. Chamberlain's enthusiastic welcome by the people of Munich on September 29, 1938,[26] as well as British intelligence reports, confirmed Chamberlain's belief that the German public desperately longed for peace.[27] However, the Munich agreement did not dispel Chamberlain's mistrust regarding Hitler's intentions.[28] Chamberlain wrote to his sister: 'We have avoided the greatest catastrophe, but we are very little nearer the time when we can put all thoughts of war out of our minds & settle down to make the world a better place'.[29] The Foreign Office concluded from the events in Munich: 'The widespread respect in Germany for the P[rime] M[inister]'s actions makes fertile ground for the dissemination of a little discreet propaganda'.[30]

Hence, the British Government decided to continue the politically hazardous German broadcasts. From September 1938 to August 1939, they aimed to inform the German public of British efforts to appease Hitler and to avert war. They sought to strengthen the desire of the Germans for peace and to arouse doubts and criticism in regard to Hitler's aggressive foreign policy. Moreover, the propaganda campaign was to warn Hitler that he would risk serious opposition from his own people if he provoked a war involving the British Empire and France and thus induce the dictator to seek a peaceful solution to his territorial claims.[31]

Although the outbreak of war destroyed the prospect of a peaceful settlement with Hitler, Chamberlain did not yet dismiss the possibility of a negotiated peace.[32] The war cut off diplomatic relations with Germany, but London continued to direct its policy—now exclusively by means of broadcasting and leaflet propaganda—at the German opposition and the German people. British propaganda now aimed to incite the Germans to revolt against their regime and to encourage them to set up a non-Nazi government with whom Britain could conclude an honourable peace and bring the war to a swift end.[33]

There can thus be no doubt that propaganda played an important role in Chamberlain's policy. Still, the British efforts to address the German public have received scant attention from both communication scholars and diplomatic historians. The campaign is briefly mentioned in studies on the BBC, on British publicity in the inter-war years, and on British propaganda during the Second World War.[34] Historians studying appeasement have generally ignored Chamberlain's efforts to communicate directly with the German people.[35] This is surprising as some of the most extensively used sources, that is, the minutes and memoranda of the British Cabinet and the archives of the Foreign Office, contain numerous references to this propaganda campaign and testify to the political significance attached to it by the Chamberlain government. One sign of its importance is the fact that it was discussed at the highest bureaucratic levels including the Cabinet and the Prime Minister himself. Hardly a week passed without some important governmental decision regarding the propaganda campaign against Germany—a pointer to its high priority on the political agenda. In December 1938, for instance, the Cabinet debated suggestions by the Foreign Office to increase propaganda in Germany.[36] And in the spring of 1939, a committee of ministers met several times to discuss measures to counter Nazi propaganda.[37]

'Straight News' or 'Propaganda'? The Negotiation of the Pre-War Propaganda Strategy between the BBC and in the Foreign Office, 1938–1939

Since Chamberlain considered propaganda an important part of his policy, and given the delicate nature of Anglo-German relations, the BBC's German-language broadcasts were put under close governmental control. However, prior to the outbreak of war, the relationship between the BBC and the Foreign Office—the government department responsible for liaison with the BBC—was of an informal nature. Both spoke of a 'gentleman's agreement' concerning their 'special contacts'.[38]

Initially, the German Service did not yet exist as a separate unit within the BBC. The news bulletins were written by the staff of the BBC Overseas Service and then translated into German and read by German translators and announcers under the supervision of the BBC Foreign Languages Supervisor. The political commentaries and talks, introduced in January 1939, were produced under the Talks Editor of the Overseas Service, Leonard Miall. For lack of a chief editor responsible for the German-language broadcasts, the Foreign Office, and later the Department of Propaganda in Enemy Countries or Department EH, as the government department responsible for British wartime propaganda was called, had thus to deal with several individuals at the BBC. Neither before, nor during the early months of the Second World War, did Whitehall exercise formal control over the output of the BBC German Service.[39]

Although the pre-war relationship between the BBC and Whitehall was informal, the Foreign Office always retained—and exercised—the right to reject or ask for the modification of a broadcast if it was not in line with the government's foreign policy aims. Often the diplomats also made suggestions as to specific themes to be taken up in the German broadcasts or insisted on the extension of the German-language programme when relations with Germany deteriorated.[40] The Foreign Office knew quite well that the BBC's Charter explicitly forbade interventions of the government and the censorship of broadcasting in peacetime. Still, the diplomats doubted the reliability of the BBC and therefore insisted on a tight control of the German transmissions.[41] In November 1938 Foreign Secretary Viscount Halifax argued 'that the relationship between ourselves and Germany was [...] delicate and that the BBC could hardly be expected to possess sufficient knowledge of the facts to enable it always to be the best judge of what should or should not be included in a bulletin'.[42]

The fact that the Foreign Office was so eager to control the German broadcasts may serve as a pointer that the primary intention of the broadcasts was not to provide the Germans for their own sake with 'straight news', but to influence them for the purposes of British foreign policy. In their internal discussions, Foreign Office officials declared that they considered the BBC German Service a propaganda instrument of the state, offered by the BBC as 'a direct service for His Majesty's Government',[43] and as a medium for countering Nazi propaganda, even if this meant deviating from the principle of strict objectivity. In January 1939 Sir Alexander Cadogan, the Permanent Under-Secretary and highest official in the Foreign Office remarked: 'As regards propaganda to Germany, I think the time has now come to go a little beyond "straight news"'.[44] Similarly, Rex Leeper urged in April 1939 that the BBC 'should indulge in direct counter-propaganda'.[45] By this the diplomats meant that the BBC German Service should develop a strategy for countering the false allegations of Nazi propaganda and for driving home to the Germans the fact that any further act of aggression against Germany's neighbours would meet with resistance.[46] However, they sought at the same time to conceal from the German listening public that the BBC German Service was closely supervised by the state, for they feared that the broadcasts would lose their effectiveness should it become known that the BBC was controlled by the government.[47]

Hence, the emphasis on the 'objectivity' of the German broadcasts in public statements by British ministers and officials, and by the BBC, should not be accepted at face value. Rather, the claim to truthfulness became part of the British propaganda strategy. In January 1939 Sir Orme Sargent, the Deputy Under-Secretary of State in the Foreign Office, in discussing the future propaganda strategy stressed that the BBC's German broadcasts should avoid evoking the impression of being propagandistic. Rather, they should appear in the disguise of impartial news to enhance their credibility. For this reason, politicians and journalists should deliberately include in their speeches and articles arguments useful to British propaganda, which could then be quoted by the BBC as objective news in their German-language bulletins.[48] In fact, the BBC instructed the German Service to reproduce in its news bulletins as often as possible the opinion of third parties or of the British public: 'This seems the right principle as it keeps both ourselves and the Government out of the picture and makes the whole atmosphere of the broadcasts more detached'.[49] Likewise, on March 15, 1939, on the day of Hitler's invasion of Prague, the Cabinet concluded that 'it was important to find language which would imply that Germany was now being led on to a dangerous path. This was of importance from the point of view of our German broadcasts which were having increasing influence'.[50]

Thus, although it is true that the BBC broadcasts differed fundamentally in tone and content from their Nazi counterparts, they were nonetheless of a propagandistic nature, aiming to transmit certain images for the purposes of Chamberlain's appeasement policy. During the last months of peace the BBC German Service pointed out the military, economic and moral superiority of Britain and its democratic system over the totalitarian dictatorship of the Third Reich. The broadcasts aimed to persuade the German people that Britain was determined to resist any further act of aggression by Hitler. At the same time they sought to counter the notion that the Western Powers wanted to encircle and attack Germany, a claim successfully brought forward by Nazi propaganda in order to rally the German people behind the regime. Instead, the BBC assured the Germans that Chamberlain was prepared to negotiate Germany's legitimate economic and territorial claims if Hitler refrained from using force.[51] In order to enhance the credibility of the German broadcasts and to stress the superiority of Britain's democracy over the Nazi dictatorship, the BBC repeatedly broadcast on the subjects of freedom of opinion and of the press, highlighting the importance of an unrestricted press for democracy.[52] When diplomatic tensions rose in the spring and summer of 1939, the BBC German Service began to dissect the falsehoods of Nazi propaganda. The talks programme regularly presented a review of the current German press, analysing topical themes in Nazi propaganda and contrasting the German claims with reports in the British press or with statements of British political leaders.[53]

Normally, the BBC willingly accepted the rule that in reporting on foreign affairs the 'national interest'—as defined by the government—had to prevail.[54] However, the archival documents bear testimony to several disputes between the BBC and the Foreign Office over the question of what constituted 'straight news' and of how to present the news without offending the Nazis. One such incident was the broadcasting of an appeal by the National Council of Labour to the German people on July 1, 1939, before it had been published in Britain.[55] In this appeal, British workers urged the German people not to accept war as inevitable, but 'to do whatever you can to make it known to your Government that you want Peace and not War'.[56] Several British newspapers reported that the BBC German Service had broadcast the Labour appeal, and they reprinted it in full length.[57] However, doubts were also raised as to the propagandistic nature of the BBC's broadcast. The *Economist* wrote:

> [The] dedication of a BBC Saturday night broadcast [...] to a pronouncement which was undoubtedly propagandist rather than completely objective is in itself significant; and there is at least a mild presumption that it was not condemned outright in Governmental circles.[58]

As could be expected, the Nazis complained to the British Embassy in Berlin about this 'moral offensive against Germany [and] intolerable interference in internal German affairs'.[59] The *Scotsman* reported that the appeal had angered official Nazi quarters who declared that 'such attempts to influence the people of the country and "seduce" them from the German Government smack of "high treason"'.[60] Contrary to the *Economist*'s assumption, however, Foreign Office officials considered the Trade Union appeal 'a great mistake and we should not approve of similar direct appeals being made'.[61] They held that direct appeals to the Germans, personal attacks on Hitler and attempts to divide the German people from the Nazis were not only ineffective but counterproductive as they were likely to unite the German people behind the regime.[62] Moreover, the Foreign Office was annoyed that the BBC had broadcast the appeal in its German-language programme before it was published in Britain and that it had failed to consult the diplomats in advance.[63] But the Foreign Office was confident that in the future similar incidents would not occur: 'We all know that the broadcasting of the manifesto was a mistake. But it's no good talking about it now and we hope to have the means of stopping similar mistakes in the future'.[64]

Chamberlain's Wartime Propaganda Strategy and Its Collapse in the Spring of 1940

On the outbreak of war, the British Government greatly intensified its propaganda campaign against Germany. In addition to the BBC broadcasts the Royal Air Force dropped millions of leaflets over the Reich. All these measures were not only aimed at informing the German people about the course of the war from the British perspective, but above all at causing a crack in the German fighting morale and at provoking an internal collapse of Hitler's regime. Britain's propaganda strategy during the 'phoney war' was based on the premise of a weak political regime in Germany and a population hostile to Nazi rule.[65] In September 1939 Chamberlain wrote:

> There is such a wide spread desire to avoid war & it is so deeply rooted that it surely must find expression somehow. [… W]hat I hope for is not a military victory—I very much doubt the feasibility of that—but a collapse of the German home front.[66]

British propaganda aimed, first of all, at increasing the doubts of the German people in the regime and its ability to win the war. The BBC German Service stressed the military, economic and moral superiority of Britain and France, and the respective German inferiority, and it predicted a speedy collapse of the German military effort.[67] In February 1940, a directive of Department EH to the BBC defined the aims of British propaganda as follows: First, to instil into the mind of the Germans doubt of victory, fear of defeat and fear of the consequences of prolonging the war (such as economic collapse and social disintegration, food shortage, Nazi excesses, air attacks and heavy losses in the army); second, to raise doubts as to the information available, and fear and resentment at being deceived; and third, to convince the German people that Germany could not win and that therefore a speedy end to the war would serve their interests.[68]

Since after the outbreak of hostilities the BBC was no longer forced to respect the political sensitivities of the Nazi regime, the broadcasts now openly called upon the German people to overthrow Hitler and to set up a non-Nazi government with whom Britain could conclude an honourable peace. A core theme of British propaganda was therefore the distinction between the German people—supposedly despising the regime and longing for peace—and the warmongering Nazis.[69] The BBC consistently used the term 'Nazi' to stress the responsibility of Hitler's regime for the war, speaking for instance of 'Nazi' merchant vessels, which had been sunk by the Royal Navy, or of the 'Nazi' war of extermination against Poland. The war was termed a 'war against Hitler', thus highlighting that Britain was not waging war against the German people, but against the Nazi government.[70]

On the outbreak of war the 'gentleman's agreement' that had hitherto governed the liaison between the BBC and the Foreign Office came to an end. The BBC German Service was put under the guidance of the Department of Propaganda in Enemy Countries, or Department EH, as it was called after its seat at Electra House in London.[71] However, the relationship between the BBC and Department EH was an organisational failure as the latter possessed little powers of control over the BBC.[72] From the beginning of 1940, Department EH issued weekly directives to the BBC German Service and occasional 'General Directives for Propaganda' concerning the treatment of specific propaganda themes.[73] But frequently those responsible for the BBC's German broadcasts (the BBC German Service as a distinct unit within the BBC did not come into existence until 1941[74]) ignored Department EH's rulings.[75] To give an example, from October 1939 onwards Department EH repeatedly asked the BBC to employ on the German programme a regular political commentator and to build him up as a 'personality speaker'. The BBC boycotted this request until February 1940, when it finally hired Lindley Fraser, a Scottish professor of economics. He spoke three times per week for 10 minutes after the late evening news bulletin and was to remain with the BBC German Service until the end of the war.[76]

To add to the organisational difficulties, news concerning the military conduct of the war was strictly censored by the Service Departments. Hence, the scope of what the BBC

German Service could actually report was meagre.[77] Although the BBC remained committed to 'telling the truth', its news reporting was severely hampered by the censorship of war news and by the over-optimistic communiqués concerning German losses and British military achievements issued by the Admiralty and the Air Ministry during the 'phoney war'.[78] This practice is illustrated by Chamberlain's letter:

> It has been a bad week with a good many losses of ships; the worst being that of the 'Rawal Pindi' (*sic*) sunk by the Deutschland with a loss of nearly 300 lives. We have known it since Thursday [23 November] but the Admiralty would not announce it, hoping that we could report the destruction of the Deutschland at the same time.[79]

Still the claims to 'truth' and 'objectivity' continued to play a key role in British wartime propaganda. A broadcast of 21 October 1939 stated: 'German citizens! If you wish to learn the truth you would be well advised to listen to the radio broadcasts from London'.[80] The BBC highlighted the advantages of Britain's democracy in which the principles of freedom of opinion and of the press were cherished and defended. Only information that was relevant to the military conduct of the war was subjected to voluntary censorship, but there existed no government department for censorship, the BBC argued.[81] Thus, the professed British press freedom served in itself as a strong moral argument; Sir Orme Sargent claimed that 'the maintenance of the liberty of the press in wartime was valuable as definite evidence that we were really fighting for the liberty of the individual in speech and thought'.[82] British propaganda also argued that the manipulation of German public opinion by Nazi propaganda posed a serious threat to world peace, and it made the re-establishment of freedom of opinion and of the press a pre-condition for peace negotiations.[83]

In their internal discussions, however, the BBC and Department EH gradually admitted that 'straight news' was a chimaera. Noel Newsome, the BBC's European News Editor, argued in February 1940: '[A]ll news and views, in addition to stimulating interest, must, however unobtrusively, serve the one and fundamental propagandist aim of helping us to win this war as rapidly as possible'.[84] Likewise, Frederick A. Voigt, the head of the Intelligence Section of Department EH, held: 'Our propaganda is not meant to entertain, enlighten or amuse the Germans. It exists not for their benefit, but for our own'.[85] Sometime later an internal memorandum of the Political Warfare Executive stated bluntly:

> It seems [...] very doubtful whether any such thing as absolute news can be provided for any audience [...]. Even the impersonal tape message has been produced by an individual reporter's choice of subject and of words and of emphasis. [...] In brief, personal factors and the limits of time or space make any such thing as absolute or 'straight' news a chimera. It is obviously in the common interest to see that the presentation and necessary modification of news which cannot be 'straight' is designed to further the end of HMG in the field of Political Warfare.[86]

Despite this rather flexible definition of what 'straight news' constituted in wartime, in the spring of 1940 British propaganda turned out to be lacking exactly its most important prerequisite—to help the government win the war. Instead, it lost credibility and persuasive power. During the Allied campaign in Norway in April and early May 1940, the BBC German Service continuously claimed British military and economic superiority while Hitler's army and navy were winning sweeping victories. The BBC could hardly be blamed for deliberately misinforming the German public, for it was dependent on the official communiqués issued by the Service Departments, and on the over-optimistic statements of Chamberlain and his ministers.[87]

At the beginning of the Norwegian campaign, Department EH predicted a speedy Allied victory: 'For the first time it can be demonstrated by British propaganda that Hitler's Germany is not invincible—a heavy blow to the Hitler legend'.[88] During the first 10 days of the campaign the BBC German Service reported self-confidently about British mining operations and air attacks on German naval bases and claimed that heavy losses had been inflicted on the invaders. It highlighted the fierce Norwegian resistance and predicted a speedy collapse of the German military offensive, arguing that the German attack on Norway had been Hitler's gravest strategic error.[89] When the Allied campaign came to a sudden halt after the heavy German bombardment of Namsos on April 20, 1940, the British Government sought to cover up the extent of the Allied losses.[90] Even after the Cabinet had decided to evacuate all British forces from Norway, the BBC continued to stress the Allies' determination to free Norway, and it reported as if the campaign was proceeding according to plan.[91] It was only on May 2 that Chamberlain publicly admitted in Parliament that the Allied forces were being evacuated.[92] Unlike the British press, however, the BBC was left in ignorance of the Allied evacuation plans until Chamberlain's speech with the result that it continued to spread optimism.[93] On May 5, Noel Newsome heavily complained about the treatment of the BBC by the Service Departments:

> [O]wing to the fact that our treatment of the campaign was based on the assumption that, although difficult, it would be carried on, a false picture of the true situation was inevitably created and, as inevitably, has had a damaging effect on our reputation abroad for reliability. [...] I should like to make it plain that any inaccurate reports which may have been broadcast concerning the Norwegian campaign have been due entirely to our treatment by the War Office.[94]

Department EH likewise blamed the Service Departments to have abused the BBC for putting out false bulletins in the hope of misleading the enemy, thus severely damaging the prestige of the BBC: 'Our propaganda will be valuable only in so far as it is true and if our news is contaminated at its source we shall rapidly get into a position in which our news will no longer be believed'.[95]

Still, after the Norwegian campaign the BBC German Service not only suffered a loss of credibility. The campaign moreover exposed the fallacy of Chamberlain's propaganda strategy that had grounded on a whole host of illusionary assumptions about the Nazi state and the German people. British propaganda had been based on the premise that the German people, even though living under a dictatorship and having no personal liberty and political rights, would cherish similar political ideals of democratic participation and responsibility as British subjects. The British Government had assumed that the Germans would sooner or later become tired of Hitler's regime and demand personal and political liberties and peace.[96] Opposite to British assumptions, however, Hitler did not care about German public opinion—and hence the German people did not possess political weight within the Nazi state. The majority of the German people were not opposed to the Nazi regime. Rather, most Germans were apathetic and politically uninterested, and they even agreed to a large extent with Hitler's foreign policy and military successes. In fact, Hitler's popularity reached its peak in the years 1938–1940.[97] The spring of 1940 thus did not see the long-awaited internal collapse of the Third Reich. Rather, the Allied defeat in Norway and the beginning of the German offensive in Western Europe brought to light the flaws in the British propaganda strategy and the fallacy of Chamberlain's hope for a German revolution. After the fall of France in June 1940, the BBC admitted that its strategy, as agreed with Department EH, had failed. Hitler's victories had rendered the arguments of British propaganda implausible because they contradicted the reality experienced by the German audience. Hence, the BBC's reputation as a credible source of information had been damaged:

> On one major point after another, [the BBC's] confident assertions have been belied—the impossibility of Hitler maintaining his expedition in Norway, the certainty that he would suffer from his foolhardiness in braving the British command of the seas; the invincibility of the Allied troops in the Netherlands, the incapacitating fatigue of the German troops, the solidarity of the Anglo-French entente; lastly, the impregnability of the Maginot line and the unyielding temper of the French. On all of these major points the German propaganda has vindicated its boasts, and British news has been proved wrong. It is not reasonable to expect that Germans can now have much confidence in the interpretation of events offered by the BBC.[98]

Likewise, the Foreign Office concluded that no form of propaganda would have any effect on the Germans unless they were beginning to suffer military defeats and severe economic hardships[99]: 'The time for propaganda is not ripe. It will only come later on, when we have got the Germans properly on the run. Till then it is, in my opinion, wasted effort'.[100] This amounted to no less than the admission that one important pillar of Britain's military strategy, that is, the attempt to demoralise the German public by way of propaganda and to incite them to revolt against their Nazi rulers, had failed.

Still, to give up the propaganda campaign and to cease broadcasting to the German public never was an option for the British Government. After the fall of France, Britain was in a desperate strategic situation. Despite having lost all continental allies during the German *Blitzkrieg* campaigns, London decided to continue the struggle against Germany alone, although it was more than doubtful whether Britain could win the war without help from outside.[101] In view of Hitler's victories in western Europe, no one in London now seriously hoped for an immediate internal collapse of the German home front. The new Prime Minister, Winston Churchill, left no doubt that he intended to defeat Germany on the battlefield and not by way of propaganda.[102] Even so, Churchill never contemplated discontinuing the propaganda campaign. In view of her military inferiority, Britain needed to make use of all available means—including propaganda and subversive warfare.[103] Moreover, with the Nazis' proclamation of a 'New European Order' after the defeat of France, Britain faced a serious propaganda challenge that called for British counter-proposals for the post-war reconstruction of Europe.[104]

The BBC German Service and Department EH (which underwent a series of reorganisations during 1940–1941 and merged into the Political Warfare Executive[105]) quickly overcame their initial shortcomings. By ruthlessly reporting Britain's initial military drawbacks as well as later her victories,[106] the BBC German Service was able to (re)build its reputation as a truthful and credible source of information which prevails until this day. Mansell has argued that its strength 'lay in the respect it gained among Germans for the accuracy of its news, [...] the calmness of its speakers, the matter-of-fact tone in the commentaries, which made such an enormous contrast to the hectic shouting [...] of the Nazi broadcasts'. But then, Mansell also admits that the 'BBC's unchallenged reputation in Germany' was 'painfully and patiently built up throughout the war years'.[107]

Conclusion

From the first day of its existence, the BBC German Service served the political aims of Chamberlain's government. During 1938–1940 propaganda played a central role in London's appeasement policy and warfare directed towards Nazi Germany, and the BBC became the most important channel for conveying British propaganda to the German public. Since its foundation, the Corporation had internalised the proposition that broadcasting had to serve the 'national interest' and, with few exceptions, did not challenge the view that in relation to foreign affairs it was the government who defined the 'national interest'. Given the particularly tense period in Anglo-German relations during 1938–1940, it is not surprising that the Foreign Office (and later Department EH) sought to bring the BBC under its control. Although the BBC and the Foreign Office occasionally held conflicting views in regard to the German broadcasts, these occasions were rare, and generally there was a great measure of agreement between the BBC and Whitehall as to the propaganda strategy to be adopted.

Although the Corporation had a reputation for reporting truthfully and objectively and being a public service broadcasting service independent of government control, the historical record shows that 'truth' and 'objectivity' were rather flexible paradigms that served different purposes. On the one hand, BBC and government officials widely used these concepts in their public statements. They believed that public knowledge of government control of the BBC German Service would jeopardise the credibility of the broadcasts as a source of truthful information and thus reduce the effectiveness of British propaganda. On the other hand, 'truth' and 'objectivity' became themselves important claims of British propaganda, serving to enhance the credibility of the British broadcasts in the ears of the German listeners.

Yet, during the 'phoney war' the BBC's German broadcasts gradually lost their credibility. Two factors—one outside the reach of the BBC and of Department EH, the other home-made—account for the failure of Chamberlain's propaganda strategy. First, the BBC depended for its broadcasts on the news releases of the Service Departments. Often, their communiqués spread an over-optimistic picture of the military course of the war or were inaccurate. Hence, they contradicted the experience of the German audience and lost their credibility and impact. Second, Chamberlain's propaganda strategy grounded on a whole host of unrealistic assumptions about the nature of the Nazi regime and of the attitude of the German people to it that were exposed as untrue in the spring of 1940.

Following a realignment of British propaganda after the abortive Allied campaign in Norway and the fall of France, the BBC German Service did finally regain its reputation for truthfulness and credibility during the course of the war. But for a different, and more effective, propaganda strategy to evolve it needed the arrival of a new Prime Minister,

REVISITING TRANSNATIONAL BROADCASTING

Winston Churchill, to lead Britain's intransigent war effort against Nazi Germany, and the overcoming of the appeasement mentality that had characterised Chamberlains propaganda during 1938–1940.

Notes

1. "News for Foreigners." *The Listener*, December 8, 1938, 1228.
2. "The German News Broadcasts." *Manchester Guardian*, February 3, 1939, 12.
3. "News of Britain." *The Times*, March 9, 1939, 15.
4. Leeper to Trevor, March 4, 1939, The National Archives, London (subsequently cited as TNA), FO 395/626, P 635/6/150.
5. Leeper was head of the Foreign Office News Department until 1939. In October 1938 he was replaced in his capacity as Foreign Office press officer by Charles Peake and put in charge of organising a nucleus Political Intelligence Department (PID) for the collection of information of value for the British propagandists and for the British government as a whole. The PID was established as a secret Foreign Office Department at the outbreak of the Second World War and provided cover for the British wartime propaganda organisation Department EH and later for the Political Warfare Executive when that body was formed in 1941. See Taylor, *Projection*, 36–8, 276–7, 284–6); Seul, "Appeasement," 225–6; 653–7; West, *Truth Betrayed*, 38, note 45.
6. Bussemer, *Propaganda*, 12–9; Jowett and O'Donnell, *Propaganda and Persuasion*, 2, 166–70, 228–32, 239–53; Ribeiro, "Objectivity," 276.
7. Seul, "Journalists," 88.
8. Briggs, *Golden Age*, 397–410; Mansell, *Let Truth Be Told*, 40–64; Taylor, *Projection*, 181–215; Taylor, *British Propaganda*, 97–100.
9. Balfour, *Propaganda in War*, 88–102; Mansell, *Let Truth Be Told*, 64–123; Stenton, *Radio London*; Garnett, *Secret History*; Briggs, *War of Words*.
10. On journalism ethics see Ward, "Journalism Ethics"; Kaplan, "Origins of Objectivity."
11. Curran and Seaton, *Power without Responsibility*, 107–11 (quotation 111); Scannell and Cardiff, *Social History*, 108–11.
12. Curran and Seaton, *Power without Responsibility*, 113 (quotation); Scannell and Cardiff, *Social History*, 109–12.
13. Scannell and Cardiff, *Social History*, 74; Curran and Seaton, *Power without Responsibility*, 133.
14. Scannell and Cardiff, *Social History*, 73, 75–7.
15. Curran and Seaton, *Power without Responsibility*, 113–5.
16. Scannell and Cardiff, *Social History*, 101.
17. Curran and Seaton, *Power without Responsibility*, 133.
18. Ribeiro, "Objectivity."
19. On appeasement, a controversial policy to this day, and the state of research see Dutton, *Neville Chamberlain*; Self, *Neville Chamberlain*; Aster, "Appeasement"; Stedman, *Alternatives to Appeasement*.
20. Cabinet 45(38)10, September 26, 1938, TNA, CAB 23/95; "Broadcasting of News Bulletins in European Languages," BBC Written Archives Centre, Caversham, Reading (subsequently cited as BBC WAC), R 1/3/40, G.107/38, 1–2; Taylor and Pronay, "An Improper Use"; Seul,

REVISITING TRANSNATIONAL BROADCASTING

"Appeasement," 170–4. BBC copyright material reproduced courtesy of the British Broadcasting Corporation. All rights reserved.

21. Taylor, *Projection*; Taylor, *British Propaganda*; Seul, "Appeasement," 28–53.

22. Seul, "Appeasement," 58–91; Adamthwaite, "British Government"; West, *Truth Betrayed*; Cockett, *Twilight of Truth*.

23. Scannell and Cardiff, *Social History*, 82.

24. Seul, "Appeasement," 106–8.

25. Self, *Neville Chamberlain*, 295–7.

26. Neville to Hilda Chamberlain, February 5, 1939, in Self, *Downing Street Years*, 377–9.

27. Seul, "Appeasement," 181–5, 199–207.

28. Ibid., 197.

29. Neville to Hilda Chamberlain, October 15, 1938, in Self, *Downing Street Years*, 355.

30. Minute Creswell, October 15, 1938, TNA, FO 371/21665, C 12202/62/18.

31. Seul, "Appeasement," 219–30, 313–54, 430–1, 518–30; Seul, "Journalists," 89.

32. Neville to Ida Chamberlain, September 10, 1939, in Self, *Downing Street Years*, 443–6.

33. Seul, "Appeasement," 685–7, 725–6, 736–47, 1363–4.

34. Briggs, *Golden Age*; Briggs, *War of Words*; Mansell, *Let Truth Be Told*; Adamthwaite, "British Government"; Taylor, *Projection*; Taylor, "If War Should Come"; Taylor and Pronay, "An Improper Use"; West, *Truth Betrayed*; Balfour, *Propaganda in War*; Stenton, "British Propaganda"; Cruickshank, *Fourth Arm*; Wittek, *Britischer Ätherkrieg*.

35. Middlemas, Diplomacy; Watt, *How War Came*; Parker, *Chamberlain and Appeasement*; Dutton, *Neville Chamberlain*; Self, *Neville Chamberlain*; Aster, "Appeasement"; Stedman, *Alternatives to Appeasement*.

36. "British Propaganda in Germany," memorandum Halifax, December 8, 1938, TNA, CAB 24/281, CP 284(38); Cabinet 59(38)5, December 14, 1938, TNA, CAB 23/96; Cabinet 60(38)3, December 21, 1938, ibid; Seul, "Appeasement," 258–69.

37. "Ministry of Information," memorandum Hoare, June 2, 1939, TNA, CAB 24/287, CP 127 (39), 1; Cabinet 18(39)4, April 5, 1939, TNA, CAB 23/98; "Meeting of Ministers to discuss certain questions affecting propaganda in foreign countries," April 12, 1939, TNA, CAB 104/89; "Final Minutes of Second Meeting of Ministers [...]," 18th April, 1939, ibid; Seul, "Appeasement," 476–9, 585–90.

38. Warner to Phillips, November 7, 1938, TNA, FO 395/583, P 3133/90/150. On the mechanism of cooperation between the BBC and the Foreign Office in relation to the German-language broadcasts see Seul, "Journalists," 90–6.

39. Seul, "Journalists," 91–6; Seul, "Appeasement," 478–9, 619–25; Garnett, *Secret History*, 83–4; Mansell, *Let Truth Be Told*, 81, 153–6.

40. Seul, "Journalists," 91.

41. Minute Warner, October 4, 1938, TNA, FO 395/623, P 2868/2645/150.

42. Record of a conversation (Ogilvie, Graves, Halifax, Leeper), November 1, 1938, BBC WAC, E 9/12/1. See also minutes Control Board, November 8, 1938, BBC WAC, R 3/3/13, CB 675; minutes Board of Governors, November 9, 1938, BBC WAC, R 1/1/6, minute 174.

43. "Some Emergency Propaganda Measures," memorandum Leeper, April 13, 1939, TNA, CAB 21/1071, 2–3. See also Seul, "Journalists," 96.

44. Minute Cadogan, January 21, 1939, TNA, FO 371/23006, C 1931/53/18.

45. "Some Emergency Propaganda Measures," memorandum Leeper, April 13, 1939, TNA, CAB 21/1071, 2.
46. Seul, "Appeasement," 335–9, 345–6, 431–2.
47. Minute Warner, November 18, 1938, TNA, FO 395/583, P 3234/90/150; Seul, "Journalists," 97.
48. Minute Sargent, January 21, 1939, TNA, FO 371/23006, C 1931/53/18.
49. Nicolls to Director of Overseas Services, February 8, 1939, BBC WAC, E 9/12/2.
50. Cabinet 11(39), March 15, 1939, Conclusion 2, TNA, CAB 23/98.
51. Seul, "Journalists," 98. For a detailed account of the British propaganda strategy see Seul, "Appeasement," 170–4, 193–208, 219–30, 313–54, 401–535.
52. "Deutschfeindliche Propaganda. Sonderbericht [...]," February 27, 1939, Bundesarchiv Berlin, R 74/552; "List of German News Talks and Press Reviews," appendix to memo Barker, "The BBC's German News Talks," July 21, 1939, TNA, FO 395/631, P 3336/6/150, 2; Gordon Walker to Newton, February 21, 1939, BBC WAC, R 51/182/1; Gordon Walker to Newton, February 22, 1939, ibid.
53. Seul, "Appeasement," 433–5.
54. Scannell and Cardiff, *Social History*, 76–7, 87–90.
55. Seul, "Appeasement," 500–1; Seul, "Journalists," 104–5. Another instance of disagreement was the Nazi persecution of the Jews in the Third Reich, see Seul, "Any Reference to Jews."
56. Cited in Burridge, *British Labour*, 23; Seaton and Pimlott, "Struggle," 143.
57. "Labour's Appeal to the German People." *Economist*, July 8, 1939, 63; "Why kill each other." *The Times*, July 3, 1939, 8; "Nazi Views." *Scotsman*, July 4, 1939, 10; "Why kill each other." *Manchester Guardian*, July 3, 1939, 5.
58. "Labour's appeal to the German people." *Economist*, July 8, 1939, 63.
59. No. 769 Ogilvie-Forbes to Halifax, July 4, 1939; minutes Roberts, Kirkpatrick, Stevens, TNA, FO 371/22990, C 9538/16/18.
60. "Nazi Views." *Scotsman*, July 4, 1939, 10.
61. Warner to Rumbold, July 12, 1939, TNA, FO 395/630, P 2967/6/150. See also minute Roberts, July 11, 1939, ibid.; Minute Warner, June 29, 1939, TNA, FO 395/630, P 2966/6/150.
62. Note Perth summarising conversation with Henderson, July 8, 1939, TNA, FO 395/666, P 3022/2862/150; Pimlott, *Political Diary*, 288 (August 29, 1939); Seaton and Pimlott, "Struggle," 144–5.
63. Minutes Stevens and Colvin, July 14, 1939, TNA, FO 371/22990, C 9538/16/18; no. 769 Ogilvie-Forbes to Halifax, July 4, 1939, ibid.
64. Minute Kirkpatrick, July 13, 1939, TNA, FO 371/22990, C 9538/16/18.
65. Seul, "Appeasement," 729–37, 1330–5.
66. Neville to Ida Chamberlain, September 10, 1939, in Self, *Downing Street Years*, 445.
67. Seul, "Appeasement," 839–70.
68. "Memorandum from Department EH to the BBC on Broadcasts in German," February 25, 1940, BBC WAC, R 34/639/3, 5–6.
69. Seul, "Appeasement," 756–99; Balfour, *Propaganda in War*, 167–70.
70. Seul, "Appeasement," 773–4.
71. Garnett, *Secret History*, 10–5; Balfour, *Propaganda in War*, 89–90; Seul, "Appeasement," 612–9.

72. Balfour, *Propaganda in War*, 89–91; Garnett, *Secret History*, XXIII–XXIV, 18–21; Seul, "Appeasement," 619–25.
73. "Memorandum from Department EH to the BBC on Broadcasts in German," February 25, 1940, BBC WAC, R 34/639; "EH/PID/PWE German and Austrian Intelligence. Recollections of A.R. Walmsley," January 20, 1946, TNA, FO 898/547, 7.
74. Mansell, *Let Truth Be Told*, 155.
75. Seul, "Appeasement," 619–25; Garnett, *Secret History*, 18–21.
76. "The Twenty-Fifth Meeting of the Planning and Broadcasting Committee held on Wednesday, October 11th, 1939," TNA, FO 898/7, Minute 13; "A Special Meeting of the Planning and Broadcasting Committee on the occasion of Mr. Ogilvie's visit, held on Saturday, 17th February, 1940," TNA, FO 898/7, 2; "Propaganda in Enemy Countries," draft memorandum Stuart, May 26, 1940, TNA, FO 898/3, 9; "Publicity in Enemy Countries," memorandum Stuart, February 12, 1940, TNA, CAB 68/5, WP(R)(40)55, 2; "German News Commentator—Professor Lindley Fraser," memorandum Barker, January 30, 1940, BBC WAC, R 13/148/1; Garnett, *Secret History*, 18–9; Briggs, *War of Words*, 181–2; Mansell, *Let Truth be Told*, 152; Seul, "Appeasement," 1020, note 268.
77. Briggs, *War of Words*, 147, note 1, 191–4; Mansell, *Let Truth Be Told*, 66–9; Taylor, *British Propaganda*, 169; Seul, "Appeasement," 877.
78. Balfour, *Propaganda in War*, 160–1, 172–3; Seul, "Appeasement," 876–7, 1256–8.
79. Neville to Hilda Chamberlain, November 26, 1939, in Self, *Downing Street Years*, 473.
80. "Daventry, 13.30 Uhr, deutsch (Mittagsmeldung)," monitoring report of 'Sonderdienst Landhaus', October 21, 1939, Bundesarchiv Berlin, R 74/337, 32–33 (author's translation).
81. Seul, "Appeasement," 821–3, 875, 877–8.
82. TNA, FO 371/28692, quoted in Cockett, *Twilight of Truth*, 138.
83. "The 104th Meeting of the Planning and Broadcasting Committee held on Saturday, 3rd February, 1940," TNA, FO 898/7, minute 9e; Seul, "Appeasement," 1042–3.
84. "Presentation of European News Bulletins," memorandum Newsome, February 12, 1940, BBC WAC, E 2/138/1, 1.
85. Memorandum Voigt for Planning Committee of 1 June, May 31, 1940, TNA, FO 898/3, 3.
86. "Draft Reply to Mr. Newsome's Memorandum of 9th December," December 10, 1941, TNA, FO 898/41, 2–3.
87. Seul, "Appeasement," 1228–37.
88. "Special Propaganda Flights to Germany," memorandum Stuart, April 18, 1940, Imperial War Museum London, Stuart Papers, 334, 2–3. See also memorandum Stuart, "The Urgency of Leaflet Propaganda to North German Towns at this moment," April 16, 1940, ibid.
89. Seul, "Appeasement," 1222–3, 1236–40.
90. War Cabinet 99(40)4, April 21, 1940, TNA, CAB 65/6; War Cabinet 100(40)3, April 22, 1940, TNA, CAB 65/12 (Confidential Annex); Seul, "Appeasement," 1242–3.
91. BBC broadcast, April 24, 1940, Deutsches Rundfunkarchiv, Frankfurt-on-Maine, tape no. 82 U 3876; BBC broadcast (6.60 a.m.), April 27, 1940, ibid., no. 82 U 3880; BBC broadcast (2.30 p.m.), April 27, 1940, ibid., no. 82 U 3878; Seul, "Appeasement," 1246–53.
92. Butler, *September 1939–June 1941*, 140; Seul, "Appeasement," 1254–6.
93. Seul, "Appeasement," 1250–2, 1256–7.
94. "European News," memorandum Newsome, May 5, 1940, BBC WAC, R 28/58/1.

REVISITING TRANSNATIONAL BROADCASTING

95. "Notes for Ministry of Information Meeting, May 17th, 1940," unsigned, TNA, FO 898/5, 1–2.
96. Seul, "Appeasement," 1330–2.
97. Kershaw, *Hitler Myth*, 156; Seul, "Appeasement," 1330–5.
98. "Monthly Intelligence Report. Europe (excluding Spain and Portugal)," July 8, 1940, Churchill Archives Centre, Churchill College Cambridge, Newsome and Ritchie papers, NERI 3/8, 6.
99. Minutes Roberts, Makins, Vansittart, April 25, 1940, 2 May 1940, TNA, FO 371/24412, C 57/150/18.
100. Minute Young, April 24, 1940, TNA, FO 371/24412, C 57/150/18.
101. Reynolds, "Churchill and the British Decision"; Reynolds, "1940: Fulcrum."
102. Seul, "Appeasement," 1287–9.
103. Stenton, *Radio London*; Stafford, *Britain and European Resistance*; Stafford, "Detonator Concept."
104. Seul, "Europa im Wettstreit"; Seul, "Appeasement," 1288–9, note 227.
105. Garnett, *Secret History*; Balfour, *Propaganda in War*, 88–102.
106. Mansell, *Let Truth Be Told*, 90–91, 157; Briggs, *War of Words*, 9–10.
107. Mansell, *Let Truth Be Told*, 163–4.

References

Adamthwaite, Anthony P. "The British Government and the Media, 1937–1938." *Journal of Contemporary History* 18, no. 2 (1983): 281–297. doi:10.1177/002200948301800206.

Aster, Sidney. "Appeasement: Before and After Revisionism." *Diplomacy and Statecraft* 19 (2008): 443–480.

Balfour, Michael. *Propaganda in War, 1939–1945: Organisations, Policies and Publics in Britain and Germany*. London: Routledge and Kegan Paul, 1979.

Briggs, Asa. *Golden Age of Wireless. Vol. 2 of the History of Broadcasting in the United Kingdom*. Oxford: Oxford University Press, 1965.

Briggs, Asa. *The War of Words. Vol. 3 of the History of Broadcasting in the United Kingdom*. Oxford: Oxford University Press, 1970.

Burridge, Trevor D. *British Labour and Hitler's War*. London: Andre Deutsch, 1976.

Bussemer, Thymian. *Propaganda: Konzepte und Theorien* [Propaganda: Concepts and Theories]. With a foreword by Peter Glotz. 2nd ed. Wiesbaden: VS Verlag für Sozialwissenschaften, 2008.

Butler, James R. M. *September 1939–June 1941. Vol. 2 of* Grand Strategy. 2nd ed. London: HMSO, 1971.

Cockett, Richard. *Twilight of Truth: Chamberlain, Appeasement and the Manipulation of the Press*. London: Weidenfeld, 1989.

Cruickshank, Charles. *The Fourth Arm: Psychological Warfare 1938–1945*. London: Oxford University Press, 1977.

Curran, James, and Jean Seaton. *Power without Responsibility: Press, Broadcasting and the Internet in Britain*. 7th ed. London and New York: Routledge, 2010.

Dutton, David. *Neville Chamberlain*. London: Arnold, 2001.

Garnett, David. *The Secret History of PWE: The Political Warfare Executive 1939–1945*. With an Introduction and Notes by Andrew Roberts. London: St Ermin's Press, 2002 [originally written 1945–1947].

Jowett, Garth S., and Victoria O'Donnell. *Propaganda and Persuasion*. 5th ed. Los Angeles, CA and London: Sage, 2012.

Kaplan, Richard. "The Origins of Objectivity in American Journalism." In *The Routledge Companion to News and Journalism*, edited by Stuart Allen, 25–37. New York and London: Routledge, 2010.

Kershaw, Ian. *The 'Hitler Myth': Image and Reality in the Third Reich*. Oxford: Oxford University Press, 1987.

Mansell, Gerard. *Let Truth Be Told: 50 Years of BBC External Broadcasting*. London: Weidenfeld and Nicolson, 1982.

Middlemas, Keith. *Diplomacy of Illusion: The British Government and Germany, 1937–1939*. London: Weidenfeld and Nicolson, 1972.

Parker, R. A. C. *Chamberlain and Appeasement: British Policy and the Coming of the Second World War*. London: Macmillan, 1993.

Pimlott, Ben, ed. *The Political Diary of Hugh Dalton 1918–1940, 1945–1960*. London: Jonathan Cape, 1986.

Reynolds, David. "Churchill and the British 'Decision' to Fight on in 1940: Right Policy, Wrong Reasons." In *Diplomacy and Intelligence during the Second World War: Essays in Honour of F.H. Hinsley*, edited by Richard Langhorne, 147–167. Cambridge: Cambridge University Press, 1985.

Reynolds, David. "1940: Fulcrum of the Twentieth Century?" *International Affairs* 66, no. 2 (1990): 325–350. doi:10.2307/2621337.

Ribeiro, Nelson. "Objectivity versus 'Toxic Propaganda': The Case of Transborder Broadcasts to Portugal during World War II." *Interactions: Studies in Communication and Culture* 3, no. 3 (2012): 275–287. doi:10.1386/iscc.3.3.275_1.

Scannell, Paddy, and David Cardiff. *A Social History of British Broadcasting: Volume One 1922–1939: Serving the Nation*. Oxford: Basil Blackwell, 1991.

Seaton, Jean, and Ben Pimlott. "The Struggle for 'Balance.'" In *The Media in British Politics*, edited by Jean Seaton and Ben Pimlott, 133–153. Aldershot: Ashgate, 1987.

Self, Robert, ed. *The Downing Street Years, 1934–1940. Vol. 4 of the Neville Chamberlain Diary Letters*. Aldershot: Ashgate, 2005.

Self, Robert. *Neville Chamberlain: A Biography*. Aldershot: Ashgate, 2006.

Seul, Stephanie. "Appeasement und Propaganda 1938–1940: Chamberlains Außenpolitik zwischen NS-Regierung und deutschem Volk [Appeasement and Propaganda, 1938–1940: Chamberlain's Foreign Policy in Relation to the National Socialist Government and the German People]." PhD diss., European University Institute, Florence, 2005. http://cadmus.eui.eu/handle/1814/5977.

Seul, Stephanie. "Europa im Wettstreit der Propagandisten: Entwürfe für ein besseres Nachkriegseuropa in der britischen Deutschlandpropaganda als Antwort auf Hitlers 'Neuordnung Europas', 1940–1941 [Rival Blueprints for Post-War Europe: British Efforts to Counter National Socialist Propaganda on the 'New European Order', 1940–1941]." *Jahrbuch für Kommunikationsgeschichte* 8 (2006): 108–161.

Seul, Stephanie. "'Any Reference to Jews on the Wireless Might Prove a Double-edged Weapon': Jewish Images in the British Propaganda Campaign towards the German Public, 1938–1939." In *Jewish Images in the Media*, edited by Martin Liepach, Gabriele Melischek, and Josef Seethaler, 203–232. Vienna: Austrian Academy of Sciences, 2007.

Seul, Stephanie. "Journalists in the Service of British Foreign Policy: The BBC German Service and Chamberlain's Appeasement Policy, 1938–1939." In *Journalists as Political Actors: Transfers and Interactions between Britain and Germany since the Late 19th Century*, edited by Frank Bösch and Dominik Geppert, 88–109. Augsburg: Wißner, 2008.

Stafford, David. "The Detonator Concept: British Strategy, SOE and European Resistance after the Fall of France." *Journal of Contemporary History* 10, no. 2 (1975): 185–217. doi:10.1177/002200947501000201.

Stafford, David. *Britain and European Resistance 1940–1945: A Survey of the Special Operations Executive, with Documents*. Toronto, ON: University of Toronto Press, 1980.

Stedman, Andrew David. *Alternatives to Appeasement: Neville Chamberlain and Hitler's Germany*. New York: I.B. Tauris, 2011.

Stenton, Michael. "British Propaganda and Raison d'État 1935–1940." *European Studies Review* 10 (1980): 47–74.

Stenton, Michael. *Radio London and Resistance in Occupied Europe: British Political Warfare 1939–1943*. Oxford: Oxford University Press, 2000.

Taylor, Philip M. *British Propaganda in the 20th Century: Selling Democracy*. Edinburgh: Edinburgh University Press, 1999.

Taylor, Philip M. *The Projection of Britain: British Overseas Publicity and Propaganda, 1919–1939*. Cambridge: Cambridge University Press, 1981.

Taylor, Philip M. "'If War Should Come': Preparing the Fifth Arm for Total War." *Journal of Contemporary History* 16, no. 1 (1981): 27–51. doi:10.1177/002200948101600103.

Taylor, Philip M., and Nicholas Pronay. "'An Improper Use of Broadcasting…' The British Government and Clandestine Radio Propaganda Operations against Germany during the Munich Crisis and After." *Journal of Contemporary History* 19, no. 3 (1984): 357–384. doi:10.1177/002200948401900301.

Ward, Stephen A. "Journalism Ethics." In *The Handbook of Journalism Studies*, edited by Karin Wahl-Jorgensen and Thomas Hanitzsch, 295–309. New York and London: Routledge, 2009.

Watt, Donald Cameron. *How War Came: The Immediate Origins of the Second World War, 1938–1939*. London: Heinemann, 1989.

West, William J. Truth *Betrayed*. London: Duckworth, 1987.

Wittek, Bernhard. *Der britische Ätherkrieg gegen das Dritte Reich: Die deutschsprachigen Kriegssendungen der British Broadcasting Corporation* [Britain's Radio War against the Third Reich: The German-language War Broadcasts of the British Broadcasting Corporation]. Münster: C.J. Fahle, 1962.

BBC PORTUGUESE SERVICE DURING WORLD WAR II
Praising Salazar while defending the Allies

Nelson Ribeiro

This article analyses the editorial line of the BBC Portuguese Service during World War II, presenting evidence of how the output of the broadcasts was influenced by the need of the Foreign Office to maintain a good relationship with the authoritarian regime led by Oliveira Salazar. Focusing on the internal guidelines that ruled the Service, this history demonstrates how Portuguese language broadcasts never threatened the survival of the regime that ruled in Portugal, despite the fact that towards the end of the war the station was used as a weapon to pressure Salazar to give in to British demands, namely to end exports of tungsten to Germany. A discussion is presented on the difficult task the Portuguese Service had to accomplish throughout the war: to praise a dictatorship while promoting British views on the war.

The BBC broadcasts to Portugal started in June 1939 after insistent requests from the British Embassy in Lisbon that urged the creation of a broadcasting service targeted at Portugal. Its purpose was to counter-attack the German propaganda campaign that was very well structured in the country, with operations extending from broadcasting to the exhibition of posters in strategic squares and the publication of brochures targeted at different publics. Well aware of the effective work that the Germans were doing on the propaganda front in Portugal, the British Ambassador in Lisbon, Sir Walford Selby, issued several alerts regarding the low profile of the work being carried out by the British in this field and, at the end of 1938, requested that the Foreign Office put pressure on the BBC to broadcast, at the very least, a regular news bulletin to Portugal.[1]

Influencing Portuguese public opinion became indeed a critical area of focus for all foreign propaganda services operating in Portugal. The country was then ruled by a dictatorship led by Oliveira Salazar, known as the *Estado Novo* (or New State), with close ideological connections with the Axis dictatorships, meaning that individual rights were limited, namely the freedom of speech (Azevedo 1999; Carvalho 1973; Gomes 2006). In fact, censorship was enforced on all local media with the result that the Portuguese showed a huge interest in listening to broadcasts from abroad. This interest would become even more visible after the start of World War II. Although Portugal maintained a neutral position, the censorship apparatus always ensured that the local press and radio stations would give a moderated picture of war developments. As a consequence, major military achievements were suppressed or their publication was delayed for a few days, meaning that those listening to foreign radio stations were, on many occasions, the first to be made aware of significant military advances (Ribeiro 2011, 254–60).

On the British side, besides counter-attacking German propaganda, in the months preceding the war, getting the message across to the Portuguese public was particularly important for two main reasons. First, the *Estado Novo*'s ideological connections to the continental authoritarian regimes made it possible for some sections of the Portuguese elite to advocate a closer relationship with Germany, which the British wanted to avoid. On the other hand, London was well aware of Franco's proposal to Salazar to sign a Treaty of Non-Aggression. This proposal, which was submitted in September 1938 to the Head of the Portuguese Government, was very well received by the British authorities. Besides establishing that no attack should be launched against Spain from Portuguese territory and vice versa, the proposed text also mentioned Franco's intention of remaining neutral if war should break out in Europe. After pressure from the Foreign Office, Salazar signed the treaty in March 1939, giving Portugal the role of 'an intermediary between Spain and the western democracies' (Telo 1998, 138).

Against this background, Sir Walford Selby considered broadcasts by the BBC to be essential for strengthening propaganda activities in Portugal, especially as the Germans had been transmitting in Portuguese since 1936 and were then way ahead of the British in regard to radio propaganda. Nevertheless, and despite its late start, the BBC quickly established itself as the most listened to foreign station with the highest credibility in the country, a status that can be explained by three main reasons. The first was the pro-British sentiment existing at that time in Portuguese society, namely inside the *Estado Novo*, which even led Salazar to present the Portuguese neutrality in the context of the Portuguese–British alliance (Rosas 1994, 303). A second reason was the employment by the BBC of a well-known announcer of the Portuguese state broadcasting service, Fernando Pessa, whose style of presentation was widely appreciated. Lastly, but also crucial, was the BBC's strategy of self-promotion as 'the voice of truth' (Ribeiro 2011, 318–20). In fact, while the transmissions from Berlin received low credit for airing mostly blatant propaganda, the BBC gained high credibility as it presented itself as being objective and truthful.

Even though the broadcasts from London were one of the main sources of information in Portugal during World War II, little research has been conducted on the topic until now. The general historiography of the *Estado Novo* oscillates between not mentioning the London transmissions and describing episodic cases in which news aired on the BBC had some influence over Salazar (Rosas 1994; Telo 1991). Most works dedicated to the history of Portuguese media and propaganda during the 1930s and 1940s do mention the BBC, commenting on the high numbers of listeners (Barros 1993; Ribeiro 2005; Telo 1990). But they do not analyse how it shaped listeners' views on the war, nor do they comment on how broadcasts were perceived by Portuguese society and how they were used as a weapon of war by the British authorities.

The first study assessing the role of the BBC in Portugal during World War II was published in 2011. It detailed the context that led to the emergence of the BBC Portuguese Service, described its internal organisation and analysed listener reactions to the transmissions (Ribeiro 2011). Previous research has also focused on how Salazar managed to influence those employed and dismissed from the Portuguese Service

(Ribeiro 2010). Therefore, this article aims to present an analysis of the editorial line of the broadcasts to Portugal focusing on how the BBC was used as a weapon of soft diplomacy by following the directives of the Foreign Office, which was determined to maintain good relations with Salazar for most of the war.

The research presented here is based on archival documents from the National Archives (with focus on the Foreign Office material), the BBC Written Archives Centre, the Portuguese Historical-Diplomatic Archive and the Portuguese National Library. The latter holds a collection of scripts aired in 1944/1945 by the Portuguese Service. Reports on internal discussions that took place inside the BBC and the Foreign Office regarding the editorial policy of the Portuguese Service are used as sources as well as listeners' comments on the BBC's editorial options. The paper argues that despite the fact that the majority of those who listened to broadcasts from London believed they were listening to an unbiased source, the Service clearly followed the directives of the Foreign Office and therefore presented a broadly supportive picture of Salazar's regime.

Relations with Salazar

From the start of the broadcasts, the BBC Portuguese Service made great effort not to create bad relations with the *Estado Novo*. Besides guaranteeing that the Portuguese political exile Armando Cortesão,[2] who had been employed by the BBC, would not play an important role in the broadcasts,[3] just a few days before the inauguration of the Portuguese transmissions, on 30 May 1939, the Empire Service transmitted a talk by Charles Martelli, in which the good relationship between the British and Portuguese Governments was highlighted:

> The recent exchange of messages between Dr. Salazar and Mr. Chamberlain are particularly gratifying to the British public. Portugal is the most ancient ally of Britain and it is pleasant to think that the friendship which unites the two countries has not only survived unimpaired for nearly six centuries but is actually more firmly established today than ever.[4]

Besides providing a synthesis of the history of the alliance between the two countries, Martelli explained the reasons that led Britain and Portugal to have different positions on the Spanish Civil War in an attempt to legitimise Salazar's good relations with Franco. This is just one example of the amount that was done by the BBC to continue their good relationship with Salazar and his regime despite its ideological connections with the Axis. In fact, during World War II the broadcasts from London frequently flattered the Lisbon Government, which was perceived by the British authorities as a means of preventing the *Estado Novo* from taking measures against the circulation of British news and propaganda in Portugal. It seemed clear that the best strategy to maintain some freedom of action in the promotion of British views on the war would be to set them in a context of praise for Salazar, as this was something highly appreciated by the Portuguese dictator (Ribeiro 2011, 267, 278).

As early as February 1939, a committee appointed by the British Ambassador in Lisbon to study the importance of the BBC broadcasts to Portugal made it clear that flattering the Lisbon regime should not be forgotten by the new foreign service that the BBC was preparing to launch:

> The news bulletins should comprise a daily survey of world news, and in particular
> include items dealing with Portuguese affairs which would have important 'flattery' value.
> In this connection the Press Attaché is prepared to supply by telegraph, or by mail when
> possible, suitable items to the News Department of the Foreign Office, to be forwarded
> to the Overseas News Editor of the British Broadcasting Corporation.[5]

The Lisbon Embassy soon became aware of the importance given by the local authorities to news concerning Portugal that was published or broadcast in the British media. For that reason, in the month that preceded the inauguration of the broadcasts to Portugal, the Press Attaché of the British Embassy in Lisbon, Marcus Cheke, mentioned in a letter addressed to the Foreign Office some of the initiatives he would undertake in order to assure that the new Service would cultivate good relations with the *Estado Novo*. This would include him furnishing important news to be aired on the transmissions to Portugal, for instance 'Salazar's birthday or the anniversary of the foundation of the New State' as well as 'local news items'.[6] Cheke, who had begun to be considered pro-Salazar in London, wanted the BBC to focus on 'straight news, stories of British war heroism, ridicule of Hitler and the Nazis which implied no carry-over to the Portuguese Government, and descriptions of British justice' (Cole 1987, 91).[7]

Even though no diplomatic incident was provoked by the BBC broadcasts to Portugal during the first year of the war, the British authorities remained very concerned about not criticising the *Estado Novo*. In December 1940, Sir Ronald Campbell, who then served as British Ambassador in Lisbon, expressed some discomfort with the content of the broadcasts and advised the BBC to be cautious when addressing issues that could be viewed as unpleasant for the Lisbon Government. In one of his first letters to the Foreign Office, Campbell suggested it was thus very important to counter-attack the main lines of attack of German propaganda, namely that Britain would impose democracy in Portugal and overthrow Salazar and his regime.[8]

The Ambassador considered it crucial for the BBC to deny these accusations, which then led him to write to William Strang, an Assistant Under-Secretary of State in the Foreign Office. He suggested that the best way to put an end to the speculation would be to publicise a transcript of the 'Question and Answer' session in the House of Commons of 23 January 1941, where the Secretary of State for Foreign Affairs guaranteed that the British Government would not interfere in Portuguese internal affairs and considered all ideas being disseminated to the contrary as a propaganda manoeuvre. Furthermore, in 1941, when the Portuguese Service added talks to its regular schedule, the Ambassador advised the Foreign Office to ensure that the word 'democracy' was avoided on these new programming features.[9]

It was a very difficult period for the Portuguese Service, as it had to balance the defence of British values with the need not to create any diplomatic incident with Salazar. On several occasions talks regarding international current affairs, which had been broadcast on other European services, had to be edited for transmission on the Portuguese Service. Social instability or disturbances that took place in Portugal were also not mentioned on a number of occasions, a fact that was criticised by listeners, especially since the BBC usually reported such events taking place in Portugal on the Spanish Service:

I heard this talk by 'Costa Abrantes' in Spanish and afterwards in Portuguese in the evening, but the Portuguese text was not equal to the Spanish, especially where reference was made to the small countries who wish to continue to ignore the existence of Russia.[10]

Many of those who listened to the Spanish Service tended to prefer it because 'it was more caustic'.[11] This appeared to be a normal reaction since, on the Portuguese broadcasts, besides democracy and social instability in Portugal pieces on communism and news from the Soviet Union were sometimes avoided. Since the *Estado Novo*'s ideology was totally anti-communist and Salazar had identified the Soviet regime as the main threat to humankind, in the local press and radio all the news from Moscow was blocked out by the censors. Aware of this situation, after the German invasion of the Soviet Union, initiated in June 1941 and which led Portuguese pro-German sections of opinion to become more active, Sir Ronald Campbell advised the BBC to be very cautious about the transmission of news from Russia and even protested against the importance given in the broadcasts to the arrival of a Russian mission in London during July 1941:

> BBC radio newsreel this morning 8.00 a.m. described the arrival of the Russian mission in London, at which the crowd broke through the barrier in their enthusiasm waving red flags and giving the salute of the clenched fist. To give this out publicly seems to be in direct contradiction to the policy and attitude laid down in Governmental declarations. Is it necessary to broadcast these things to the world? So far as this country anyway is concerned it will lead to immediate and marked cooling of Anglo-Portuguese relations.[12]

Campbell's concern with Salazar's reaction was not at all unjustified. The Head of Government was very well informed of the content of the broadcasts and also of the internal routines and discussions that took place at the Portuguese Service. This was possible since the Embassy in London maintained good relations with some employees inside the Section, some of whom were Portuguese civil servants whose stay in London had been authorised by Salazar himself, following a request from the Ministry of Information.[13] Moreover, Colonel Egerton, who in 1941 became a regular author of talks aired on the BBC, in addition to being an admirer of the *Estado Novo*, was also known to maintain contact with the Portuguese Ambassador in London, Armindo Monteiro. Among other initiatives that illustrate his loyalty to the Lisbon regime, he published a book in 1943 called *Salazar, the Rebuilder of Portugal*.

New Guidelines, the Same Concern

In October 1941, relations between Lisbon and London were troubled by the 'Armando Cortesão crises', during which the Portuguese authorities were made to believe that Cortesão, despite being a political exile and considered an enemy of the *Estado Novo*, would be put in charge of the BBC's Portuguese Service. Although all evidence points to the fact that this was nothing more than a rumour, Salazar responded in a very robust way, suppressing all news of British origin from the press. This was, in fact, the most dramatic incident of the power relationship between the BBC and the Portuguese Government, which ended with the dismissal of Cortesão from the Corporation in

November of that same year following pressure exercised by the Foreign Office and the Ministry of Information (Ribeiro 2010).

Following this crisis, the Foreign Office was even more concerned about the policy that should be followed regarding the broadcasts to Portugal. The matter was discussed in a meeting on 7 November 1941 in which a 'Guideline for Broadcasts to Portugal' was produced that defined the main objectives of the Service as follows:

> The basic object of our broadcasts to Portugal is to present the war through British eyes, to convince the Portuguese of the justice of our cause, to show that our institutions and our ways of life are to be admired, to bring home to the listener that whilst a German victory would mean the dismemberment of the Portuguese Empire by the Axis powers, a British victory which the support of our friends will hasten is a guarantee of the integrity and independence of Portugal and her Empire.[14]

It was then considered that news bulletins should be 'factual and objective in tone', and that no news item with news value should be excluded just because it was believed that it would be embarrassing to Salazar. Nevertheless, the guidance given to those working at the Portuguese Service was to avoid selecting items that would be 'gratuitously offensive to the Portuguese Government or Portuguese listeners or which could be interpreted as interference in Portuguese internal affairs'.[15]

Since the fight against communism was a political priority for the *Estado Novo*, it comes as no surprise that the German invasion of the Soviet Union, initiated in June that year, was well received by conservative sectors in Portugal. Therefore, in order not to further damage relations with Lisbon, the BBC gave instructions to its Portuguese Service to broadcast only necessary news about Russia, focusing on the military achievements and avoiding comments on the Soviet internal system:

> We should not attempt to gloss over the extent of our own and American assistance to Russia, but we should exclude references to such things as demonstrations at which the participants raised their clenched fists in honour of Maisky, playing the Internationale in England, laudatory references to the Soviet social system, statements that the Soviet Government grants religious freedom to Soviet citizens.[16]

On the other hand, the Portuguese Service was advised to pay particular attention to news items that would help make it clear that, despite the British support for Russia in the war against Germany, the British Government was not supporting the communist system. For this reason it was considered important to include items such as the refusal of the Home Secretary to remove the ban on the *Daily Worker*, the official organ of the Communist Party.

In news concerning the American continent, the new guidelines produced for the Portuguese Service advised it to pay attention to Latin America, particularly Brazil, because North America was not considered popular in Portugal. 'In particular, great care should be taken in treating United States references to the Portuguese Atlantic Islands'.[17] Regarding talks, the instructions aimed to ensure that these would project Britain and its way of life. It was also considered important to comment on the developments of war and the flattery of Salazar and his regime was once more recommended even though the BBC was quite cautious, warning of the lack of efficiency that praise without suitable grounds would have among listeners:

As in all other European Services, one of our main purposes, and the most difficult, is to project Britain. [...] In talks, as well as in the news, we can and should praise Salazar for any act of the Portuguese Government which calls for praise. Flattery of Salazar without a peg on which to hang it, pounded out merely for the sake of flattery, is insincere and to be deprecated.[18]

The new guidelines adopted by the Portuguese Service were an attempt to reconcile the Foreign Office's interest of maintaining good relations with Salazar with the need not to give away on the BBC's editorial ideal of reporting objective news. Furthermore, one must also take into account that the recommendations mentioned above were given to the Portuguese Service during what can be considered one of the tensest periods in the relationship between the two countries. The negotiations concerning a plan for the Lisbon Government to retreat to the Azores in the event of an Axis invasion continued to reach no consensus, due to two main points of divergence. The first concerned the timing in which Portugal should abandon its neutral position in the war. Salazar wanted it to take place only in the event of direct aggression against Portugal, while the British wanted it to take place as soon as the Germans attacked the Iberian Peninsula. Second, it also proved to be difficult to reach an understanding on the extent of destruction to be carried out in Portugal in order to make it more difficult for the Germans to use strategic infrastructures (Rosas 1994, 307–8).

'The Shell Network' and Its Impact on the Editorial Line

Despite all the diplomatic tensions that existed between Lisbon and London during the first years of the war, the BBC never adopted a tone of attack against the Lisbon Government, not even during the dismantlement of the Special Operations Executive's (SOE) information network by the Surveillance and State Defence Police (PVDE). This case, which came to be known as 'The Shell Network', was a real headache for the British during 1942 and made the Allies' propaganda efforts in Portugal more difficult than ever (Barros 1991; Telo 1990).

It all started during the previous year when the SOE, without informing the British Embassy in Lisbon, decided to create an extensive network of contacts among the Portuguese, including sympathisers of the clandestine Communist Party and anarchists. The aim of the network was twofold:

in the event of a German invasion it would carry out a widespread plan to demolish strategic installations, and then stay behind to form the nucleus of a future guerrilla movement to provide resistance against the occupying forces, with possible support from the UK. (Telo 1990, 102)

The network was based on previous MI6 contacts in the opposition and also on contacts provided by employees of the oil company Shell and the staff of other British companies operating in Portugal.

In January 1942, following information most likely received through the Spanish political police (Telo 1990, 102) and the German Embassy (Wylie 2006, 168), the PVDE started to arrest several Portuguese members of the network and later on became aware of the involvement of British citizens working for Shell. This was, of course, exploited by

German propaganda in Portugal. A communiqué stating that 'the English network was linked to the communists and it intended to overthrow the Government' (Telo 1990, 103) appeared. The British Embassy, which had started out by not giving any attention to the incident, later on had to officially regret it and downplay its importance. Simultaneously, Sir Ronald Campbell protested to the Foreign Office that in order to avoid incidents like 'The Shell Network', the Embassy should be made aware of all contacts being made in Portugal. Furthermore, following the Portuguese authorities' request, the British Ambassador would demand that the SOE's Head of station, Jack Beevor, should leave his post (Telo 1990, 104; Wylie 2006, 168). This did indeed occur in June 1942, putting an end to most of SOE's activities in Portugal (Barros 1991; Murphy 2007, 204).

The dismantling of the network was followed by the expulsion of two British citizens from the country, and by the arrest of several Portuguese nationals also involved. Despite representing a humiliation for the British, the Embassy's collaboration with the PVDE continued to be considered satisfactory. The political police,

> immediately released four Portuguese nationals who were only involved in distributing propaganda, and in June others were released, while Campbell assured Salazar that no explosives were distributed, only radios and signalling pistols. Nonetheless, the British 'abandoned' the Portuguese nationals most clearly culpable, who would end up receiving custodial sentences. (Telo 1990, 104)

During this difficult period, the BBC never attacked either Salazar or his government. Moreover, in November 1942, after the signature of a supply-purchase and a war trade agreement between the two countries, the British Ambassador advised the BBC to be very cautious when addressing this subject so as not to create any problems with Salazar who was constantly obsessed with maintaining the image that Portugal's sovereignty was not negotiable in any way:

> Press Attaché is anxious to make some propaganda of conclusions of Supply-Purchase and War Trade Agreement, and suggests that press announcements [...] when made should be supplemented by explanatory statement or 'talk' on the BBC Portuguese broadcast. I see no objection to this provided that it is done discreetly and due account is taken of Doctor Salazar's susceptibilities about 'sovereignty' and 'collaboration'. Any such 'talk' should show that benefits expected from Agreement are mutual. Text would have to be very carefully prepared in conjunction with Ministry of Economic Warfare.[19]

The caution expressed by Campbell in the telegram quoted above is consistent with the attitude that the BBC always took when Salazar was concerned. This was, of course, not well received by those opposing the *Estado Novo* and led them to frequently protest against the editorial line of the Portuguese Service. As was the case of an anonymous writer from Coimbra:

> [The Portuguese Service has never broadcast] even lightly, any criticism of the Fascist system and of the atrocities and persecutions practised by the Portuguese Government. [...] Nor [...] have we heard the slightest hope given to listeners that after the victory of the United Nations, the rights of the citizen, liberty of the press, and democracy for which the people of Portugal are wholeheartedly yearning will be brought into being in Portugal.[20]

In January 1943 the Foreign Office approved a new propaganda plan for Portugal drawn up by the Ministry of Information. It clearly shows a continued British concern not to cause any discomfort to Salazar and his regime and foresees the need of the BBC to highlight that an Allied victory would not have any effect on the internal political organisation of Portugal. To start with, the plan states that the propaganda to Portugal should 'convince the Portuguese of the certainty of United Nations victory with special emphasis on Britain's vital contribution' clarifying that the defeat of the Axis would not 'mean communism or social upheaval in Portugal' rather, on the contrary, it would bring benefits to the Peninsula. On the other hand it was also stated that propaganda should also 'convince certain groups that an Axis victory would mean disaster for them' and that religion would be destroyed by an Axis victory, but would 'prosper through the victory of the United Nations'.[21]

As for relations with the *Estado Novo*, the plan suggested that British propaganda should convey the idea that the Portuguese Government was respected by Britain and that the 'collapse of European fascism would not mean the end of the New State'.[22] Also, important to Salazar was the provision of assurances that the propaganda would stress that the Allies had no designs whatsoever on the Portuguese colonies. Nevertheless, during the last two years of the war, the BBC's editorial line underwent a subtle shift, starting in the months that followed the signature of the Azores agreement in August 1943, an agreement that granted the Allies access to military facilities (Rosas 1994, 316–7; Telo 1991, 154–63). The BBC would reinforce the amount of news and talks concerning Russia and, later on, would start to air features addressing democracy and the exports of tungsten from Portugal to Germany (Ribeiro 2011, 2013). This would, of course, be bad news for the *Estado Novo*.

The Change of Tone after the Azores Agreement

During the last quarter of 1943, even before the Azores agreement was publicly announced, the BBC began to adopt a different attitude towards the *Estado Novo*. On the one hand it did not confront the regime; on the other hand it did broadcast news and talks about international policy defending values that were not accepted by Salazar. The most visible case was Russia.

Although the local media continued to portray Moscow as a threat to humankind, following Germany's severe losses on the Eastern front the BBC did not hesitate to broadcast news about developments on the Russian front and to talk about living conditions in the country. The Soviet Union was presented mostly on favourable terms. Two examples were the talks entitled 'The Truth about Bolshevism' and 'The Church and Russia' which were aired on September 1943.[23] In the following months BBC listeners also had the opportunity to listen to other talks about Russia and its role in the war.

The Portuguese export of tungsten to Germany was another controversial issue addressed on the Service. Portugal, from the beginning of the war and despite its neutral position, was an important supplier of tungsten to the German forces. Even during the final period of the military conflict, Salazar delayed as much as he could in giving into British demands to put an end to this trade (Rosas 1994, 318–22).

In January 1944, the Minister of Information assured Parliament that the BBC was taking steps to acquaint the Portuguese people with the dissatisfaction felt in the UK on account of Portuguese exports of tungsten to Germany.[24] The topic would be first addressed on the transmissions to Portugal on 10 April when the BBC transmitted a warning by the American Secretary of State, Cordell Hull, to the neutral countries. The inclusion of passages of Hull's speech on the Portuguese Service marked the beginning of a new tone. During April and May 1944, when Allied victory seemed likely, the BBC frequently referred to the British and American attitude on the supply of tungsten and other raw materials to Germany,[25] namely on the *Monday Chronicle* series that became a central feature of the Portuguese Service during the final period of the war. The *Monday Chronicle* was authored by António Pedro, a Portuguese surrealist writer and painter who joined the BBC in January 1944. Some of the talks that addressed the issue of tungsten exports were 'Nazism versus Neutrality', aired on 17 April, 'The Position of Neutrals' (24 April) and 'Liberty and Intervention' (8 May).[26] Furthermore, the gold sent to Lisbon by the Germans to pay for the supply of tungsten was also mentioned in the broadcasts. Thus, in July 1944 the BBC reported the arrival 'of a shipment of German gold, which had been transported to Portugal from Switzerland' (Lochery 2011, 199).

Other topics addressed by Pedro also illustrate the change in editorial policy of the BBC towards Portugal. Even though Pedro had been a member of the fascist movement *Nacional-Sindicalista* in the early 1930s, when he arrived in London his political beliefs had changed and he confessed his admiration for the British parliamentary system. As early as January 1944 Pedro spoke about the House of Commons, describing it as the 'backbone of British politics and the Areopagus of its democracy'.[27] The following month, he would once more use events taking place in Britain to speak about the democratic system. Despite the fact that the *Estado Novo*'s propaganda was then presenting democracy as a regime not suitable for Portugal and considered not to be able to respond to the real needs of contemporary societies, this did not prevent Pedro from extolling its virtues:

> Democracy. What does this so reviled word really mean? [...] The British democracy is more than a regime, more than a way of thinking put into action—it is a form of being. The Englishman has his social life organised in a series of brackets that end at the royal palace. English life is based on a series of social strata ranging from the factory worker and the farmer to the House of Lords. But all of them, Lords and factory workers have the same duties and have the same rights in society. But all of them, lords and factory workers can move up or down the social ladder according to their conduct. [...] What there is absolutely no doubt about is that for a society to organise itself and function to the point where it is possible to have a Churchill and a British people coinciding in action because they mutually represent one another, it is essential that there is complete, equal, and total freedom of thought and expression.[28]

Although it is clear that Pedro's strong political views could not always be expressed in the terms he considered most suitable, it is also true that his arrival at the Portuguese Service coincided with a particularly critical period in the relationship between London and Lisbon. This made it possible for him to speak about themes that displeased the *Estado Novo*, which, before then, had not been addressed on the Portuguese Service. From the beginning of 1944, the British Government applied pressure on Salazar to stop the export of tungsten to Berlin (Rosas 1994, 319; Telo 1991, 230). The BBC was used as one of the means to exercise that pressure which lasted until June 1944, when the agreement that ended the exports to Germany was finally announced (Ribeiro 2011, 294–5).

After 'D-Day', democracy would continue to be a core topic along with criticism of the fascist regimes. Professor Castillejo's talk on 13 July, entitled 'In Search for a Regime for Italy', can be taken as an example to illustrate the kind of language the BBC used during the last year of the war:

> Fascism is the dictatorship of a party, the persecution of minorities, the transformation of universities and schools into an instrument of political propaganda. […] It is condemnation without citation of the legal infraction. It is the retroactive application of punishment, arbitrary fines, capricious taxes, intolerance as a banner, aggression as a method, with imperialism as a bait. […] For Italy to choose her government and for that government to be the expression of the national life, the legal protection of all citizens must first be guaranteed. No-one must live condemned to silence, nor at the unbridled mercy of police and lawless authorities.[29]

According to the Broadcasting Officer in Lisbon, this kind of talk created in the pro-democratic listeners the sense that after the war Britain would 'step in and establish a democratic regime in Portugal'.[30] The same can be said about the *Monday Chronicles*. Even though Pedro had to face the obligations imposed on the BBC's editorial line not to directly criticise the government of Salazar, he would take advantage of every pretext to indirectly expose the dictatorial nature of the *Estado Novo* and disseminate the concept of parliamentary democracy which led to these weekly talks becoming 'the most listened to and discussed feature'[31] during the second half of 1944.

Although towards the end of the war the editorial line of the Portuguese Service became less agreeable to the *Estado Novo*, Salazar's regime was in fact never seriously threatened. Even where the exports of tungsten to Germany were concerned, instead of openly attacking Salazar the Portuguese Service criticised the 'neutral countries'. On the other hand, despite the focus on fascist regimes, the BBC never openly stated that it considered the *Estado Novo* to be one of those regimes. Furthermore, although several talks on democracy were aired in 1944, and were severely criticised by the Lisbon regime and the local conservative press,[32] the BBC never openly stated that democracy should be implemented in Portugal. On the contrary, as the end of the war became foreseeable, the British Government chose to maintain good relations with Salazar and support his continued hold on power. As a result, talks that could represent a threat to Salazar's regime were dropped and some texts by Pedro had several paragraphs cut in 1945, especially those which were focused on democracy or that criticised the Iberian dictatorships. For example, the following comment on British foreign policy was simply not allowed:

> Whichever party wins the election (and it is not easy to foresee who will), Britain's foreign policy will be a call to all European countries to lead a worthy political life, based on democratic principles and understanding with America and with Russia.[33]

After the end of the war, Pedro's presence at the microphone would become inconvenient for the Corporation. He was then told that it was now a matter of policy that the BBC 'should not make broadcasts of a kind that would be thought by the Portuguese listeners to constitute an interference in their own affairs',[34] even when it was clear that a large section of the audience would applaud such interference. The Acting Controller of European Services, Harman Grisewood, spoke with Pedro on 10 October 1945 and made it clear that this was a non-negotiable matter since it was creating an embarrassing situation for the British Government.[35] As a consequence, Pedro tendered his resignation on 22 October, while the BBC continued to broadcast to Portugal, avoiding confrontation with the Lisbon regime. In the following year, both the British and the Americans would give their support to the dictatorship by backing Portugal's application to become a member of the United Nations (Rosas 1994, 399).

Conclusion

During 1939–1945, the BBC Portuguese Service never seriously threatened either Salazar or his regime. On the contrary, during most of the war the BBC broadcasts to Portugal flattered the *Estado Novo* in accordance with the Foreign Office's strategy of keeping good relations with Salazar. This was considered very important due to Portugal's geographic position and to the influence it could have on Spain's neutrality.

The British Embassy in Lisbon frequently advised that the BBC should avoid items that would annoy the Lisbon regime, namely communism, democracy and social disturbances in Portugal. Serving as Minister of Information for a brief period at the start of World War II, between 4 September 1939 and 5 January 1940, Lord Macmillan's initial outlines of British wartime propaganda policy well described the broadcasts to Portugal. He held the view that foreign broadcasts should 'respect susceptibilities of certain countries'[36] which was in fact the case of the Portuguese Service that during the war struggled to combine the respect for Salazar's susceptibilities with the defence of British political beliefs.

The cordial tone that the Portuguese Service adopted towards the *Estado Novo* only suffered a visible change in the last quarter of 1943. On the one hand, the Service continued to avoid direct confrontation with the Portuguese regime, but, in contrast, it also started to include regular talks on the Soviet Union, which were not well received by Salazar. Nevertheless, it was only in 1944 that the BBC adopted a tone that was annoying to the Portuguese regime, when it started airing talks on democracy and on the export of tungsten to Germany by neutral countries. However, to the disappointment of all those who wished for a regime change to take place in Lisbon, the broadcasts from London never directly attacked Salazar's regime nor did they mention its connections with the Axis regimes that were about to be defeated.

Throughout the war, the Portuguese Service clearly followed the directives of the Foreign Office and Ministry of Information, produced in order to align the broadcasts with the diplomatic strategy followed in each period. Therefore, the content of the transmissions was adapted to the aims determined by the British Government, exercising more or less pressure on Salazar as and when the Foreign Office deemed most appropriate. It must not be forgotten that during the war, and despite the existence of several different phases, the Corporation was under the scrutiny of the Ministry of Information, which led the Governors of the BBC to reaffirm that after the war all foreign language services under their control would be 'objective and non-propagandist' (BBC 1946, 7). Nevertheless, this was not the case during the war. Even though the Foreign Office did use the broadcasts in the final period of the war to pressurise the Portuguese regime to end exports of tungsten to Germany, British diplomacy constantly demanded that the BBC maintain a flattering or at least non-threatening tone towards Salazar in order to avoid retaliations that could lead to restrictions on British propaganda activities in Portugal at the time. This strategy adopted by the British clearly did not serve the purposes of the internal opposition in Portugal and therefore helped the *Estado Novo* to extend its existence after the end of the war. In fact, even though World War II saw the victory of democracy over authoritarianism, in Portugal a democratic regime would only be implemented almost three decades later following the Carnation Revolution of 1974.

Funding

This work was supported by the Research Centre for Communication and Culture (CECC) at the Catholic University of Portugal, financed by the National Science Foundation FCT under the project PEst-OE/ELT/UI0126/2013.

Notes

1. Minutes from the Foreign Office, January 1939, The National Archives, Kew, London (subsequently cited as TNA), FO 395/625.
2. Known for his opposition to the *Estado Novo*, Cortesão was convicted in absentia in 1934 for the attempted overthrow of Salazar. He was among a group of more than one thousand anti-fascist Portuguese of the political and military elites who sought exile in Spain before going to Britain (Oliveira 1996, 263–5).
3. Historical Diplomatic Archive, Lisbon (subsequently cited as AHD), M.97 CP and M.248 CP.
4. Charles Martelli, "Food for Thought—Portugal", broadcast on the Empire Transmission II, 30 May 1939, AHD, M248 CP and M97 CP.
5. Report from February 1939, TNA, FO 395/625.
6. Letter from Marcus Cheke to the News Department (FO) 11 May 1939, TNA, FO 395/628.
7. Starting the previous year, Marcus Cheke's work had been considered less than satisfactory in London (Cole 1987, 52).
8. Letter from Sir Ronald Campbell to William Strang (F.O.), January 1941, TNA, FO 371/26818.
9. Letter from Sir Ronald Campbell to William Strang, 12 May 1941, TNA, FO 371/26818.
10. "BBC Survey of European Audiences—Portugal", 30 October 1943, BBC Written Archives Centre, Caversham, Reading (subsequently cited as BBC WAC), E2/198.
11. Ibid, 9 October 1944, BBC WAC, E2/198.
12. Telegram from Sir Ronald Campbell to the Foreign Office and Ministry of Information, 9 July 1941, TNA, FO 371/26818.
13. Letter from Director of the Foreign Publicity Directorate (Ministry of Information) to Armindo Monteiro, 10 September 1939, AHD, M 97 CP.
14. BBC internal document "Guideline for Broadcasts to Portugal", 7 November 1941, TNA, FO 371/26819.
15. Ibid.
16. Ibid.
17. Ibid.
18. Ibid.

19. Telegram from Sir Ronald Campbell to FO, 10 December 1942, TNA, FO 371/31113.
20. "BBC Survey of European Audiences—Portugal", 16 May 1944, BBC WAC, E2/198.
21. Plan of Propaganda for Portugal, 14 January 1943, TNA, FO 371/34691.
22. Ibid.
23. "BBC Survey of European Audiences—Portugal", 30 October 1943, BBC WAC, E2/198.
24. *Hansard*, 26 January 1944, HC Deb vol. 396 cc.669–70.
25. "BBC Survey of European Audiences—Portugal", 1 August 1944, BBC WAC, E2/198.
26. Ibid.
27. *Monday Chronicle*, 31 January 1944, script in Portuguese National Library, Lisbon, Esp E5/366–366A.
28. *Monday Chronicle*, 14 February 1944, script in Portuguese National Library, Esp E5/366–366A.
29. "BBC Survey of European Audiences—Portugal", 9 October 1944, BBC WAC, E2/198.
30. Ibid.
31. "BBC Survey of European Audiences—Portugal", 15 December 1944, BBC WAC, E2/198.
32. "Ecos e Notícias. A Campanha da B.B.C.", *A Voz*, 1 October 1944.
33. *Monday Chronicle*, 18 June 1945, in BBC WAC, L1/112.
34. Memo of a conversation between Grisewood and Pedro, 10 October 1945, BBC WAC, L1/112.
35. Ibid.
36. Note by Ogilvie on Macmillan's speech delivered to the Advisory Council of the Ministry of Information, 9 September 1939, quoted in Briggs (1970, 170).

References

Azevedo, Cândido de. *A Censura de Salazar e Marcelo Caetano* [The censorship of Salazar and Marcelo Caetano]. Lisboa: Caminho, 1999.

Barros, Júlia Leitão de. "O Caso Shell." *História* 147 (1991): 55–83.

Barros, Júlia Leitão de. *O Fenómeno de Opinião em Portugal* [The phenomenon of opinion in Portugal]. Lisboa: s.n., 1993.

Briggs, Asa. *The War of Words. Vol. 3 of the History of Broadcasting in the United Kingdom*. Oxford: Oxford University Press, 1970.

BBC. *BBC Year Book 1945*. London: BBC, 1946.

Carvalho, Alberto Arons de. *A Censura e as Leis de Imprensa* [Censorship and press laws]. Lisboa: Seara Nova, 1973.

Cole, Robert. *Britain and the War of Words in Neutral Europe 1939–1945: The Art of the Possible*. London: Macmillan, 1990.

Egerton, Frederick Clement. *Salazar, Rebuilder of Portugal*. London: Hodder & Stoughton, 1943.

Gomes, Joaquim Cardoso. *Os Militares e a Censura: A Censura à Imprensa na Ditadura Militar e Estado Novo (1926–1945)* [The military and censorship: Press censorship during the military dictatorship and the Estado Novo (1926–1945)]. Lisboa: Livros Horizonte, 2006.

Lochery, Neill. *Lisbon: War in the Shadows of the City of Light, 1939–1945*. New York: Public Affairs, 2011.

Murphy, Christopher J. "SOE's Foreign Currency Transactions." In *The Politics and Strategy of Clandestine War: Special Operations Executive, 1940–1946*, edited by Neville Wylie, 191–208. London: Routledge, 2007.

Oliveira, César de. "Cortesão, Jaime." In *Dicionário do Estado Novo* [Dictionary of the Estado Novo], Vol. 1, edited by Fernando Rosas and J. M. Brandão de Brito, 228–229. Venda Nova: Bertrand, 1996.

Ribeiro, Nelson. *A Emissora Nacional nos Primeiros Anos do Estado Novo (1933–1945)* [The state broadcaster during the initial years of the Estado Novo (1933–1945)]. Lisboa: Quimera, 2005.

Ribeiro, Nelson. "Salazar's Interference in the BBC Portuguese Service during World War II." *Journalism Studies* 11, no. 2 (2010): 257–269. doi:10.1080/14616700903217471.

Ribeiro, Nelson. *BBC Broadcasts to Portugal during World War II: How Radio Was Used as a Weapon of War*. Lewiston; NY: Edwin Mellen, 2011.

Ribeiro, Nelson. "António Pedro: The Voice of Democracy in the BBC Portuguese Section during World War II". *Portuguese Cultural Studies* 5 (2013): 70–90.

Rosas, Fernando. "O Estado Novo". In *História de Portugal* [History of Portugal], Vol. 7, edited by José Mattoso. Lisboa: Editorial Estampa, 1994.

Telo, António José. *Propaganda e Guerra Secreta em Portugal 1939–1945* [Propaganda and secret war in Portugal 1939–1945]. Lisboa: Perspectivas & Realidades, 1990.

Telo, António José. *Portugal na Segunda Guerra 1941–1945* [Portugal in the Second World War 1941–1945], Vol. 1. Lisboa: Veja, 1991.

Telo, António José. "As Relações Peninsulares num Período de Guerras Globais (1935–1945) [The peninsular relations in a period of Global Wars (1935–1945)]." In *Portugal e a Guerra Civil de Espanha* [Portugal in the Spanish Civil War], edited by Fernando Rosas, 133–151. Lisboa: Colibri, 1998.

Wylie, Neville. "SOE and the Neutrals." In *Special Operations Executive. A New Instrument of War*, edited by Mark Seaman, 157–178. London: Routledge, 2006.

PAWNS IN A CHESS GAME
The BBC Spanish Service during the Second World War

Gloria García González

The Spanish Service was established in June 1939, two months after the end of the civil war in Spain and shortly before the start of the Second World War. Its implementation was strongly affected by these conflicts in the context of new international relations. Therefore, this study of the Spanish Service during 1939–1945 allows not only a better understanding of the communicational strategies developed by the BBC, but also of the complex Anglo-Spanish relations and the important role played by the Spanish-language broadcasts therein. The study is mainly based on archival documents from the National Archives in London and memoirs.

Introduction

In the context of a strong expansion of BBC European radio broadcasting, the launch of the Spanish Service responded to the particular interest the British Government had for weakening the influence of Hitler's Germany on such a strategic area of the Mediterranean as that occupied by Spain. In fact, Great Britain's relationship with this country had been conditioned since the civil war by Germany's decisive participation in favour of Franco's forces. Thus, at the end of the civil war in 1939 and in face of an imminent conflict of a greater magnitude in Europe, the British Government decided to precipitate the launch of a BBC service directed to Spain with the intention of gaining an audience for the Allied cause and thus to counteract the pro-Nazi stance of Franco's government.

For this reason, the study of the BBC Spanish Service in those years requires a complex focus on political, diplomatic, communicative as well as personal variables with the objective of unravelling the Web of political and professional interests which were woven around the radio in those years. With this aim, it has been necessary to make use of the official documents from the War Cabinet and the Foreign Office, such as the memoirs of principal protagonists in this historical time frame: Winston Churchill, Samuel Hoare, Tom Burns and Rafael Martínez Nadal. This study has been addressed chronologically with the aim of clarifying the roles of the various agents in the consolidation of the Spanish Service and their use as an efficient weapon of war at the service of the different interests deployed within the establishment in order to obtain the victory over Germany. Despite the interest in this relatively unknown dimension of British foreign policy, the Spanish Service has still not been sufficiently researched nor mentioned in the literature, apart from partial references in memoirs and works of a general character.

The Policy of Appeasement and the Restraint on Foreign Broadcasting

Once radio developed sufficiently in the 1930s, it became an essential accessory in practical diplomacy, obliging statesmen to pay more attention than ever to national and foreign broadcasting and to the effects of their policy over it.[1] However, until 1938, the policy of appeasement towards the Nazi regime led Great Britain to favour a broadcasting strategy based on prudence and contention.[2] For this reason, the BBC abstained from sending correspondents to the civil war that broke out in Spain in July 1936, in which Germany participated immediately by sending troops, aviation and armament to the rebels. R.T. Clark, the BBC News editor, waited to see its development before deciding to send one of his best journalists, Richard Dimbleby, to the Pyrenees border to report on the tragic end of the war through the eyes of nearly half a million hungry and freezing refugees crossing the border to France.

The BBC's decision to stay away from the conflict did not apparently coincide with the extraordinary interest the outbreak of this war had provoked in British public opinion and among most of the staff, but rather with the political strategy of the Foreign Office which considered the civil war as an 'internal affair' of Spain.[3] Apparently, the BBC received abundant pressure to adopt a neutral position in the conflict. Lexical recommendations were issued by the Foreign Office News Department on how to avoid the term 'rebels' and how to replace it with the softer idiom 'insurgents' when referring to Franco's troops. The insistence became so annoying to the BBC's staff that R.T. Clark urged the General Director, Sir Frederick Ogilvie, to demand from the Foreign Office that the pressure be ceased.[4] Even so, the BBC ended up assuming that the civil war was an untouchable affair in all areas of programming except in the news bulletins which were supplied exclusively by agencies.

Hence, as far as foreign broadcasts were concerned, the main impediment to news was the aforementioned policy of appeasement, given that neither Baldwin nor Chamberlain ever wanted any type of confrontation with Germany as a result of foreign language broadcasts. The only exception was the inauguration in January 1938 of broadcasts in Arabic destined to counteract the Italian influence in North Africa and the Middle East. Two months later, the BBC introduced services in Portuguese and Spanish to South America with the aim of neutralising the German economic and cultural influence in Latin America. Thus, a nucleus of foreign-language broadcasts was beginning to develop which later became known as 'Radio London'.[5]

Only a few individuals dared to support the idea of disseminating propaganda to contain the German influence in Europe. One of them was Anthony Eden, a self-declared enemy of the policy of appeasement who, as Foreign Secretary, warned that 'we have daily experience of what we may expect to suffer if we leave the field of foreign public opinion to our antagonists'.[6] He resigned in February 1938, precisely at the time when the situation in Europe was about to convulse. In March 1938, Germany annexed Austria and in September Edouard Daladier and Neville Chamberlain signed the Munich Agreement with Hitler and Mussolini in a desperate attempt to avert a war. Although there was still a great reticence throughout this year to any form of propaganda, more and more people in public office dared to support a defensive propaganda strategy against the seemingly almighty German propaganda, namely Duff Cooper, Brendan Bracken, Hugh Dalton,

Noel Newsome and Ivone Kirkpatrick, all of who would be called to occupy high positions in Churchill's government.[7]

Meanwhile, Sir Stephen Tallents, who held the post of Controller of Public Relations in the BBC, joined forces with Rex Leeper, the head of the Foreign Office News Department, to support the initiation of a BBC Overseas Broadcasting Service in foreign languages. Their endeavour came to fruition in 1939.[8] One of the critics of appeasement, Rex Leeper, had already been actively promoting foreign publicity activities, such as the creation of the British Council in 1934 or obtaining important grants for Reuters that had allowed it to compete with other foreign news agencies. However, the understanding between Tallents and Leeper soon broke down when Tallents suggested that in case of war, all propaganda should be put under the control of the Ministry of Information. Leeper, instead, wished to put it under the supervision of the Foreign Office.[9] At first sight, this seemed no more than a petty conflict of responsibility between ministries. However, it ended up taking on much more complex hues when war broke out and the necessity to exercise direct control over the programming and content of the BBC became more important than ever.

The Inauguration of the Spanish Service

The possibility of setting up a broadcasting service directed at Spain was suggested for the first time by members of the Foreign Office and the BBC in February 1939. These were, notably, Rex Leeper from the Foreign Office News Department, Sir Alexander Cadogan, the Permanent Under-Secretary of State at the Foreign Office, Cecil Graves, the Deputy Director General, and Sir Frederick Ogilvie, the Director General of the BBC.[10] A month later, the British Government rushed to recognise General Franco's regime without waiting for the end of the civil war and, finally, on 4 June 1939 the new service was inaugurated in the presence of the Duke of Alba, the Spanish ambassador in London, who took advantage of the occasion to praise the new regime and highlight the popularity it enjoyed in Spain. Immediately, *The Voice of Spain*, a pro-republican magazine edited in London by exiled Spaniards, denounced the fact that the BBC had acted as a propaganda platform for an authoritarian regime which was also anti-British.[11] After the civil war, Spain was in debt to the Nazi regime and therefore its probable alignment with Germany in case of war could seriously compromise the position of Great Britain.[12] Nobody ignored that the Spanish possessions in Morocco controlled the entrance to the Mediterranean and its wolfram mines would be essential in times of war.

In these circumstances, Great Britain pursued a diplomatic strategy of strengthening the relationship with Spain in order to keep it at a distance from the Axis.[13] To achieve this aim, opportune doses of pressure would have to be applied with important compensation in the form of oil, cereals and medicines.[14] In fact, it was the old strategy of the carrot and the stick in which the BBC Spanish Service could be an essential element in the problematic relationship between the British Government and the Franco dictatorship during the Second World War.

Britain was not highly considered by Spain because of the old contention over Gibraltar,[15] although the presence of Colonel Juan Beigbeder, a pro-British monarchist in the Ministry of Foreign Affairs, seems to have facilitated the relationship. Despite this fact,

Spain's declared neutrality in case of war was no guarantee.[16] The German presence in the country was a serious concern to the British.[17] Besides the German embassy in Madrid, there were also German consulates in various Spanish cities and dependencies of the Gestapo in the capital, not to mention the subtle presence of the potent German radio broadcasts. Added to all of this, there was the political control of the Falangist press funded by the German authorities as well as the Spanish radio committed to anti-Allied propaganda. The mission of the BBC Spanish Service to counter the German influence over the Spaniards seemed, from the start, clear although nearly impossible.

The Onset of the Radio Counterattack

At the outbreak of war, the BBC was put under the auspices of the Ministry of Information. However, the foreign language services came under the cautious, but efficient control of the Foreign Office.[18] After Winston Churchill became Prime Minister in May 1940, Duff Cooper was appointed Minister of Information and Sir Samuel Hoare—who had served as Home Secretary under Prime Minister Neville Chamberlain—British ambassador in Madrid.[19] Churchill knew that the BBC would play an important role as a weapon of war and thus needed to be closely supervised by the government. The activity in this field became frenetic. Duff Cooper restructured the propaganda machinery and started up the Overseas Planning Committee, directed at occupied and enemy countries, while he tried to coordinate with the Foreign Publicity Directorate, presided over by Anthony Leigh Ashton.[20]

Meanwhile, Tom Burns, a well-known editor and a Catholic like the British ambassador Sir Samuel Hoare, arrived in Madrid as British press attaché and was entrusted with organising and diversifying the propaganda activities of the British embassy. Despite the initial lack of staff and resources, he managed to get in touch with the Irish Catholic Bernard Malley and the various contacts he had built up during his 20 years stay in Spain.[21] Among Burns' first initiatives was the distribution of a printed BBC newsletter, given the fact that the circulation of the British press was prohibited in Spain. Although its content left much to be desired with its mix of ephemera, disinformation and apparent lack of concern, the demand began to grow among the openly anglophile circles of the Spanish aristocracy. The newsletters arrived from the Foreign Office, were translated into Spanish at the embassy and clandestinely distributed by groups of children, mostly from families who had suffered from reprisals.[22]

In June 1940, Anglo-Spanish relations entered a critical phase. Paris fell to the Germans on 14 June and two days later the Spanish army occupied Tangiers, violating its status in international law. Franco took advantage of the European impotence towards Germany and substituted neutrality for an enigmatic declaration of non-belligerence that appeared to encourage Hitler's plans to reach Gibraltar and control the Straits.[23] Alarmed by that, the British Government launched a three-pronged counterattack. This consisted, first, of a plan of bribes channelled through MI6 at a group of monarchist generals disaffected with Germany that would organise resistance to any German attempt to invade Spain,[24] second, of an advantageous commercial agreement to palliate hunger and with it 'to win over the masses',[25] and third, of a propaganda campaign run by the BBC about British economic aid to Spain. On 22 July 1940, in a letter addressed to Ogilvie,

Hoare warned: 'the press here is entirely German. The radio is our only hope'.[26] Two daily time slots aimed at Spain—at 12:45 and 22:00—were clearly insufficient against the crushing German programming in Spanish, and in September the British Government therefore declared its interest in raising the propaganda pressure on Spain.[27]

Tensions were increasing, and in October 1940 two worrying events indicated a probable entry of Spain in the war. On 17 October, Ramón Serrano Súñer, the chief of the Falange and an open admirer of Nazism, substituted Juan Beigbeder in the Spanish Ministry of Foreign Affairs, and on 23 October a meeting between Hitler and Franco took place in Hendaya. Shortly afterwards, Hitler invited Serrano Súñer to his private residence in Berchtesgaden where, according to Súñer's memoirs, he insisted on Spain's reticence to entering the war on account of the supplies of wheat and oil deriving from the agreements with Great Britain and the USA and the influence of British propaganda in Spain. Apparently, the Führer asked if he did not think that 'the deceiver British propaganda wasn't aimed at toppling Franco'. Serrano Súñer responded that 'we know the objectives of this propaganda and we fight it as far as possible'.[28] Pressure from the German Government did not stop there and Admiral Wilhelm Canaris, Chief of German Military Intelligence, transmitted to Franco the Führer's desire that German troops could enter Spain on 10 January 1941. Franco replied that 'for reasons presented in their time, it was impossible for Spain to enter the war on that date'.[29]

At the same time, the BBC Spanish Service underwent a profound restructuring. Resources and staff increased while the broadcasting time was expanded. Up to this point, the content was limited to daily news bulletins and talks broadcast a couple of times a week after the news. In charge of these was Douglas Woodruff, Director of the Catholic weekly *The Tablet* and a faithful agent of a small but influential sector of English Catholicism that resolutely supported Franco since the civil war. The seemingly scarce interest of the Spanish audience for his talks led William McCann, head of the Spanish Division in the Ministry of Information, to get in touch with Rafael Martínez Nadal, then professor at King's College in London, who was a monarchist and had no political connections with exiled Spaniards in England.[30]

Nadal did not hesitate to accept the invitation to broadcast talks to substitute those of Woodruff under the direct supervision of John Marks, writer and journalist with a good knowledge of Spain and its language. Both of them reported to William McCann at the Ministry of Information and were supervised in journalistic matters by Harman Grisewood, Assistant Controller of the European Division of the BBC, and Noel Newsome, Director of the BBC's Foreign News Division. Both were in their turn under the political supervision of another Catholic, Ivone Kirkpatrick, who was responsible for the BBC European Services in the Foreign Office. It was precisely Kirkpatrick who insisted to Nadal that 'The principal objective of British policy towards Spain was to maintain its neutrality'.[31] Weeks later, McCann told Nadal that 'they were going to double the time the BBC dedicated to Spain and that after the evening news there would be a special programme, *La Voz de Londres* [The Voice of London] of 15 minutes'. On 17 November, Nadal, under the pseudonym of Antonio Torres, began to broadcast from Wood Norton Hall, Evesham, the vast property that the Duke of Orleans had ceded to the government for war services where a large part of the BBC had been installed due to security reasons.[32]

With his talks Nadal pursued two objectives: first, to transmit to Spanish listeners the British point of view on the war, and second, to contribute to a better understanding between Spain and Great Britain through cultural content.[33] Quite soon, the daily talks started to be complemented by a special programme, *Comentarios Londinenses* [London Comments], transmitted on Sundays at 21:00 for 15 minutes and retransmitted on Mondays at 14:00. Each *Comentario* began with a summary of the most important war events during the preceding week. It was then followed by references to the most flagrant lies broadcast on the enemy stations and ended with a message of hope for victory over Germany.[34]

In December 1940, those responsible for the BBC agreed to reinforce the broadcasts in Spanish by incorporating the voices of other Spaniards linked to the world of culture and that were not aligned with Franco's regime. Even so, as a precaution, all of them were camouflaged behind a pseudonym. They were Alberto Jiménez Fraud, Director of the *Residencia de Estudiantes* in Madrid, his wife, the pedagogue Natalia Cossío, José Castillejo, professor of law, Alberto Onaindía, nationalist Basque priest, the folklorist Eduardo Martínez Tomer and Vicente Buylla, football commentator. Throughout the war, other British contributors such as Robert Hodgeson, British Government agent in Burgos during the civil war, and professors like Alison Peers, William Atkinson, William Trotter or Gerald Brenan were also invited to broadcast on the Spanish Service.[35]

The First Controversy over the Spanish Service

At the beginning of 1941, the Foreign Office complained for the first time about the programmes of Alberto Onaindía. It seems that his criticism of the Spanish dictatorship in the BBC broadcasts deviated from the official British line of no interference in Spanish internal affairs. From this moment onwards, in order to avoid unnecessary risks, all employees of the Spanish Service were required to sign a document committing them not to take part in any political activity linked to the republican exile.[36] The relationship with Spain passed through moments of great tension. The BBC's Spanish broadcasts therefore underwent constant interferences and the public image of Great Britain was injured daily by the Spanish radio and press which prophesised an immediate British defeat by Germany.[37]

On the realisation that the German propaganda offensive seemed to precede the military one, the concern grew in Great Britain that neutral countries would fall to Germany. In Spain, the British propaganda counteroffensive centred on three slogans: first, the threat that an Allied victory represented to Spain; second, the reminder of the British aid to the 'reds' during the civil war; and third, the accusation that only Britain was to blame for the scarcity of food due to the maritime blockade it imposed.[38] Added to the campaign to discredit Great Britain was the rumour that she was preparing an invasion of the Iberian Peninsula. *La Voz de Londres* counterattacked with two warnings. It argued, first, that the Spanish radio was spreading elaborated German hoaxes and, second, that it anticipated, contrary to what it said, a probable invasion by Germany.[39] Meanwhile, in one of his speeches, Serrano Súñer warned of the danger of Spain falling under the domain of Great Britain. In June 1941, exalted by the German incursion into Russia, the Spanish Government launched a violent publicity campaign against Great Britain, accompanied by numerous incidents and tumults in front of the embassy and the announcement that Hitler's victory was only a matter of weeks.[40]

At this point, Sir Samuel Hoare, understanding that perhaps the BBC Spanish Service broadcasts were worsening this offence, decided to formally complain to the British Government about the Spanish Service. The Minister of Information, Duff Cooper, responded violently arguing that he could not understand such a policy of appeasement towards the Franco government. In July 1941, Duff Cooper resigned. Hoare continued to insist that any reference to the civil war or even an attack or ridicule of fascism should be eliminated from the BBC broadcasts, thereby scandalising Kirkpatrick and Newsome who were offended by the hysterical objections of Hoare.[41] The truth is that the Franco authorities were relentless against the BBC broadcasts. Serrano Súñer, in particular, complained of the supposedly hostile tone of the Spanish Service towards Franco, and Hoare warned London that relations with Spain could be ruined if London did not tame the Spanish Service.[42]

On their part, the Franco government did everything possible to impede the reception of the BBC signals by means of interference. 'The BBC shows no sign of repenting', Hoare lamented,[43] and while the Foreign Office, the Ministry of Information and the BBC accused Hoare of exaggerating, the BBC was warned to contain itself. For the next three years, the internal history of *La Voz de Londres* was the story of the resistance of Anthony Eden at the Foreign Office, Ivone Kirpatrick, and nearly all the Spanish Division at the Ministry of Information, and the BBC against the intent of Samuel Hoare to censure the Spanish Service. In July 1941, Brendan Bracken was appointed new Minister of Information and despite the fear that the government would intervene in the BBC, Bracken's interventions were infrequent and limited in time.[44]

However, the Spanish Service continued to attract criticism. To the continual pressure of Hoare accusing Martínez Nadal of being leftist were added the disqualifications of *The Spanish Newsletter*, the organ of the exiled republicans in London and the accusations of crypto-fascists levelled against John Marks and Martínez Nadal by Elsa and Arturo Barea[45] before the *Fabian Society*.[46] The campaign achieved such effect that the Minister of Information appeared in the House of Commons to affirm that the BBC foreign language services, including the Spanish Service, were being revised. Meanwhile, the Spanish Falange authorities raged in their criticism of Martínez Nadal accusing him of being an extremist. Arthur Yencken, Minister of Council to the embassy in Madrid, in a burst of optimism told the British Government that the Falangist criticism against the Spanish Service and in particular against its principal announcer, Martínez Nadal, was only the result of an increased audience in Spain and, therefore, of an increased popularity of the Allied cause in this country. McCann, pre-empting renewed warnings, sent to the Foreign Office a report elaborated by the BBC intelligence department detailing the Spanish audience's support to Martínez Nadal and by extension to the Spanish Service.[47]

Meanwhile, Germany intensified its offensive political propaganda. On 15 October 1941, the German Ambassador, von Stohrer, presented a memorandum in Berlin in which, after exposing the strategic propaganda methods of England, considered absolutely necessary to reinforce the political propaganda strategy in Spain in the form of a Great Plan—*Der Spanien Grosser Plan*.[48]

The Spanish Service, an Obstacle to Appeasement?

In 1942, after the USA had entered the war and Germany had suffered the first defeats in Russia, Spanish foreign policy became completely erratic. On the one hand, Franco appeared to become more convinced that the course of the war was inclined in favour of the Allies, while the Falange with Serrano Súñer at the head radicalised their speeches and perpetrated more and more violent attacks against British interests in Spain. The interference of radio broadcasts intensified, postal packages addressed to Britons regularly arrived manipulated, British communiqués to the newspapers were never published, the deliverers of the embassy newsletter were intercepted and in Barcelona the British Consulate complained of several cases of people detained for possession of BBC newsletters.[49]

The BBC intelligence department reported that the Spanish Service 'clearly has increased its audience among Spaniards of all classes'.[50] However, this did not improve its reputation at the British Embassy in Madrid. Hoare remained convinced that the effect of the broadcasts on the Spanish Government was extremely negative and, as a consequence, abysmal for Anglo-Spanish diplomatic relations.[51] The repetitive complaints Samuel Hoare sent to London started to have their first consequences at the beginning of 1942 when, for the first time, the British Government questioned the professionalism of Martínez Nadal, star announcer of the BBC Spanish Service, and caused the resignation of John Marks, content supervisor of the Spanish broadcasts. Martínez Nadal managed to keep his job, for the time being, thanks to the support of Ivone Kirkpatrick.[52]

Noel Newsome also had his own reasons to complain. 'We are wandering off the target', he lamented in a letter to Kirkpatrick in March 1942.[53] He declared that the European Service would hereafter act according to the strategy established by the Commanding Officer and not like a group of guerrillas, without cohesion, plans or fixed objectives.[54] Meanwhile Hoare's pressure on the Spanish Service was incessant and at the end of June the British press attaché in Madrid, Tom Burns, met Martínez Nadal in the Garrick Club in London. In this encounter Burns made Nadal aware of the continual reproaches from the senior members of Franco's government against the Spanish Service who considered its programming partial and subversive.[55] The impression Nadal got from this conversation was that the insistence of Burns formed part of a diplomatic chess game with Franco's regime and that the BBC employees were no more than expendable pawns.[56]

On 4 September 1942, the BBC announced that Serrano Súñer had resigned as Minister of Foreign Affairs. The political disappearance of a figure so deeply committed to German Nazism could signal a turning point in the strategy aimed at Spain. On 18 November, a high level meeting took place at the BBC to deal with the broadcasts to Spain. Cadogan passed the results of the meeting to Ambassador Hoare. He defended the work of the BBC and sustained that despite what Hoare might think, there was close cooperation between the Ministry of Information, the BBC and the Foreign Office.[57] With this declaration of unbreakable unity, the chess game appeared to turn against Hoare and his strategy of appeasement towards Franco's regime. However, the game as well as the war continued.

Still, the declaration of internal unity put forward by Cadogan was not true, in practice, at least in the memory of Martínez Nadal who remembers that before the end of

1942 he began to notice an incipient breakdown in the Foreign Office's unity of criteria towards Spain, on which the Spanish Service relied for its editorial approach. As the risk of a German invasion of the Peninsula faded, two different approaches to understanding the relationship with Franco emerged. On one side was Sir Samuel Hoare, who favoured a policy of non-intervention in Spain's internal affairs and of allowing, at the end of the war, the survival of the Franco dictatorship. On the other side, Anthony Eden, nearly all of the Ministry of Information's staff, Ivone Kirpatrick and the entire BBC staff, along with the majority of the British population were convinced that the survival of a dictatorship in Europe would be morally incompatible with the Allied war aims, apart from being harmful to Great Britain.[58] This internal duel, unleashed at the end of 1942, persisted until May 1944 when Hoare ceased to be ambassador in Madrid. During this period, both tendencies struggled for control over what should or should not be said on *La Voz de Londres* and whether the BBC should contribute to the appeasement of Spain or, on the contrary, aim towards bringing about the fall of the Franco dictatorship.

Samuel Hoare against the Spanish Service

The clearly favourable progress of the war for the Allies in 1943 did not result in a reduced level of interest by the British Government in radio broadcasting. To the contrary, once an Allied victory over Germany seemed secure, the budget destined for the BBC was duplicated while the broadcasting time of the Spanish Service followed the upward trend which had begun in 1940.[59] All suggested that the interest in reinforcing the propaganda investment did not only depend on the necessities of war against Germany, but also on the need for Great Britain to consolidate its own European influence in the face of the steamrolling propaganda power of the USA.[60] At the beginning of 1943, the Office of War Information—the American office responsible for war propaganda—was authorised to broadcast to Spain from Algeria to assert the 'hard hand' approach of the USA to the Franco dictatorship.[61]

At the same time, the British Political Warfare Executive (PWE)[62] upheld—against Hoare's insistence—the necessity to increase the pressure by means of propaganda on Spain.[63] In this direction of distancing from Franco, William McCann, the director of the Spanish Division in the Ministry of Information, after questioning the work of Tom Burns in the embassy decided to travel personally to Madrid to reconsider the embassy's propaganda. The idea was to increase the penetration of British propaganda into the Spanish society without irritating Franco or interfering with the internal affairs of Spain.

During this time, the BBC's Spanish transmissions, and particularly those under the responsibility of Martínez Nadal, continued to stir up institutional controversy. Hoare's complaints became more insistent without evoking any favourable response from London. However, in July 1943, a decisive event occurred: the Allied landing in Sicily, which was followed by the fall of Mussolini a few months later. From this moment onwards, the governments of Churchill and Roosevelt worked together to intensify the pressure on Franco to distance Spain from Germany which, among other advantages, was still benefitting from the clandestine supply of its submarines in Spanish ports, absolute liberty of movement for its spy network on Spanish territory, and privileged control of the Straits from its consulate in Tangiers.[64]

Thus, on 17 and 25 July 1943, Antonio Torres (alias for Rafael Matínez Nadal) dedicated his talk on the Spanish Service to the Allied landing on Sicily concluding: 'In this critical hour for Europe, the oppressed peoples look hopefully at Great Britain, at the promises within the Atlantic Charter'. At this time, Torres could not foresee the political storm he was going to unleash. Samuel Hoare immediately sent a long telegram to the British Government in which he sustained that Torres' talk was all of a challenge to the Spanish regime and that 'to accept that the BBC is our official spokesperson is equivalent to doing a U turn in the policy of non-intervention in the internal affairs of this country'. He ended up recommending that 'the announcer should leave politics and speak to the Spaniards about life in our homeland and of our confidence in total victory'.[65] Nadal remembers that from this point onwards, the Foreign Office gave its unconditional support to Samuel Hoare behind Anthony Eden's back. Even Michael Williams, one of Hoares' strongest critics to date, now thought that perhaps the BBC had gone too far and that it was not unlikely that Torres talk might incite the Spaniards to follow the Italian example and bring down the Franco regime. Frank Roberts from the Foreign Office stood out in his support for the Spanish Service and suggested a meeting to clarify the editorial position. On 21 October, Grisewood suspended Nadal from his post as announcer to finally sack him on 2 November.[66]

On 1 October 1943, Franco's government officially returned to neutrality giving up the position of non-belligerence, and on 3 November it decided to withdraw the *División Azul*, the volunteer unit sent to the Russian front in 1941 in support of the *Wehrmacht*. With these gestures, Spanish foreign policy appeared to be looking for proximity to the Allies without abandoning its sympathy for the Axis in a dilettantism which unleashed an irate response from the US Government and grave concern in the British one.[67] On 25 October, Roosevelt's government demanded, via its ambassador in Madrid, that Spain put a total embargo on wolfram exports to the Axis.[68] After tough discussions with the British ambassador in Madrid, both governments decided on restricting the petroleum supply as a means of applying pressure without explicitly presenting it as such to avoid the possibility of being accused of blackmail by the Franco government. Unaware of this tactic, the BBC hurried to spread the story through its news channels. Obviously, the publicity about a supposed embargo increased significantly the difficulties in reaching an agreement with Franco,[69] and finally Hoare suggested to the Foreign Office in November 1943 that the BBC should be 'muzzled'.[70] The American ambassador, Carlton H. Hayes, remembers, however, that 'the BBC continued their news campaign noisily and vehemently to the annoyance and pain of Sir Samuel'.[71]

End of the War, End of Appeasement

In February 1944, Churchill agreed with the Spanish Government on the reduction of wolfram exports to Germany in a gesture of appeasement that for many demonstrated that the war as a fight against fascism had lost its direction.[72] Two months later, Martínez Nadal returned to *La Voz de Londres*, promising never again to utter criticism of the Franco government. On 24 May 1944, in the House of Commons, Churchill confirmed the policy of complacent detachment towards Spain thanking Franco's government for their neutrality in the war and insisting that Great Britain would not interfere with Spain's internal affairs. Thus, when on 18 June 1944, amidst the euphoria released by the Normandy landings, Martínez Nadal declared in his presentation for *La Voz de Londres* his hope that the Allied victory would lead to the restoration of democracy in the whole of Europe, he knew it would be his last broadcast. It was not even aired and that very afternoon Nadal left the

BBC for good. After he had left, he would comment that the policy shift undergone in the Foreign Office and transmitted by contagious contact to the editorial approach of the BBC meant 'the triumph of the powerful Tory right wing'.[73]

The war was in its final phase. In August 1944, having achieved his 'special mission' to keep Spain out of the war, Samuel Hoare was relieved as ambassador in Madrid. An important shift in relations with Spain occurred after the war. On 12 December 1946, the United Nations agreed on resolution 39, a unanimous condemnation of the Franco regime, and the closure of embassies. From that moment onwards, the BBC Spanish Service incorporated renowned anti-Franco voices with a new aim, to feed the desire for the restoration of democracy in Spain[74]

Conclusion

In March 1939, the Franco regime was recognised by Great Britain and in June of this same year a programme in Spanish directed towards Spain was set in motion. After the Munich Crisis in September 1938, the British rearming in the form of radio equipment was unceasing, and since 1939 the foreign broadcasts received priority importance from the Foreign Office as well as the Ministry of Information.

Although the Franco regime proclaimed a neutral stance at the outbreak of the war, this did not diminish the British concern, as in fact, a commitment of mutual support in diplomatic and economic affairs existed between Franco's Spain and Hitler's Germany, that in anytime could provide for a military intervention on Spanish soil. Samuel Hoare's appointment as Ambassador in Madrid and the reinforcement of Spanish Service broadcasts responded to the British Government's interests of implementing a special mission: to keep Spain out of the conflict and, at the same time, drawing Spain to the Allied cause, if possible. Nevertheless, discrepancies about how to achieve this objective, soon unleashed tension between Hoare and the BBC.

Since its beginnings, the Spanish Service found itself entangled in a tight mesh of intensely conflicting political interests within the British establishment. Therefore, what since 1940 appeared to be a petty personal confrontation between the ambassador, Sir Samuel Hoare, and the most noticeable announcer of the BBC Spanish Service, Rafael Martínez Nadal, represented the bigger conflict between two politically incompatible British projects in Spain. The first one was a policy of appeasement towards Franco without questioning the dictatorial nature of his regime and the second one was a plan for an Allied military intervention in Spain to depose the Franco government. Finally, Winston Churchill's speech in the House of Commons on 24 May 1944 solved the dilemma: Great Britain would not interfere in Spain's internal affairs. From this moment until 1945, the Spanish Service moderated its editorial approach assuming in a disciplined manner the policy laid down by the British Government.

Thus, the war revealed, as never before, the strategic importance of Spain for Great Britain, the relevancy of the BBC in the British establishment, the role of the Spanish exiles within the Spanish Service, the influence of the British Catholic Lobby within the apparatus of propaganda directed towards Spain and, lastly, the existence of irreconcilable factions inside the London Government and their interest in taking control of foreign broadcasts, convinced of their priceless value as a diplomatic tool.

Notes

1. Rawnsley, *Radio Diplomacy*, 6.
2. Scannell and Cardiff, *Social History*, 73.
3. Halifax to Neville Chamberlain, June 9, 1938, TNA, FO/800/323, 12–3.
4. Schlesinger, *Putting Reality*, 24.
5. Gillespie and Webb, "Corporate Cosmopolitism," 5.
6. Eden to Sir John Simon, December 23, 1937, TNA, T 161/907.S355811/03/38/1.
7. Stenton, *Radio London*, 5.
8. Ibid., 6.
9. Gillespie and Webb, "Corporate Cosmopolitism," 5.
10. Rawnsley, *Radio Diplomacy*, 16.
11. Monferrer, *Odisea en Albión*, 398.
12. Conclusions of a Meeting of the War Cabinet, April 17, 1940, TNA, CAB/65/6/40, 348.
13. Churchill, *Memorias*, 636.
14. Meeting of the Cabinet, June 21, 1939, TNA, CAB/23/100, 13.
15. Conclusions of a Meeting of the Cabinet, June 7, 1939, TNA, CAB/23/99, 307–8.
16. Conclusions of a Meeting of the War Cabinet, November 4, 1939, TNA, CAB/65/2/4, 29.
17. Alan Hillgarth to Prime Minister, September 13, 1940, TNA, CAB /66/12/12, 52–3.
18. Martínez Nadal, *Antonio Torres*, 31–7.
19. Conclusions of a Meeting of the War Cabinet, May 18, 1940, TNA, CAB/65/7/22, 168.
20. Cole, *Britain and the War*, 38.
21. Burns, *The Use of Memory*, 86–7.
22. Burns Marañón, *Papá espía*, 259.
23. Memorandum by the Secretary of State for Foreign Affairs, September 28, 1940, TNA, CAB/66/12/24, 2.
24. Spanish Neutrality. Scheme 1, 1940–1941, TNA, FO 1093/233; Spanish Neutrality. Scheme 2, 1942, TNA, FO 1093/234.
25. Hoare, *Embajador ante Franco*, 70–3.
26. Ibid., 58.
27. Future Strategy, September 4, 1940, TNA, CAB/66/11/42, 11.
28. Serrano, *Entre*, Ibid., 243.
29. Ibid., 259.
30. Martínez Nadal, *Antonio Torres*, 33.
31. Ibid., 290–1.
32. Burns Marañón, *Papá espía*, 291.
33. Martínez Nadal, *Antonio Torres*, 44.
34. Ibid., 63.
35. Monferrer, *Odisea en Albión*, 401.
36. Ibid., 400.
37. Burns, *The Use of Memory*, 104.
38. Actually, Spain was free from the blockade thanks to the *navicerts*, cargo certificates issued by the British Consulate in the port after inspection, to ensure that no war material was exportable to Germany; Moradiellos, *Franco frente*, 96.
39. See note 31 above.
40. Cole, *Britain and the War*, 75–7.

41. Briggs, *The War of Words*, 433.
42. Cole, *Britain and the War*, 94.
43. Hoare to Foreign Office, April 6 1941, TNA, FO 371/26951.8848.
44. Nicholas, *The Echo of War*, 56.
45. Arturo Barea was a collaborator with the BBC South American Service; Elsa, born as Ilse Pollack, was a translator in the BBC *Monitoring Service*, Townson, *Palabras*, 7–25.
46. Monferrer, *Odisea en Albión*, 427.
47. Martínez Nadal, *Antonio Torres*, 75–6.
48. Schulze Schneider, "Éxitos y fracasos," 202–5.
49. Hoare, *Embajador ante Franco*, 227.
50. BBC Intelligence Paper, January 1942, TNA, FO 371/31223.775.
51. Cole, *Britain and the War*, 116–7.
52. Martínez Nadal, *Antonio Torres*, 80–1.
53. Briggs, *The War of Words*, 437.
54. Stenton, *Radio London*, 37.
55. Burns Marañón, *Papá espía*, 288–5.
56. Martínez Nadal, *Antonio Torres*, 98.
57. Cole, *Britain and the War*, 117.
58. Martínez Nadal, *Antonio Torres*, 97.
59. Briggs, *The War of Words*, 440.
60. Manpower in the BBC. Memorandum by the Minister of Information, September 16 1942, TNA, CAB /66/28/44.
61. Cole, *Britain and the War*, 138.
62. The PWE was set up in August 1941 to produce and disseminate propaganda directed at enemy and enemy-occupied countries. It was staffed by propaganda agents from the Ministry of Information, from the BBC and from the Special Operations Executive (SOE). The latter was formed in 1940 to conduct espionage and sabotage, Stenton, *Radio London*, 6–14).
63. See note 61 above.
64. Moradiellos, *Franco frente*, 325–6.
65. Martínez Nadal, *Antonio Torres*, 116.
66. Ibid., 131–8.
67. The Spanish Situation, January 13, 1943, TNA, CAB/66/33/19, 1–3.
68. Hayes, *Misión de Guerra*, 269.
69. Hoare, *Embajador ante Franco*, 297.
70. Cole, *Britain and the War*, 139.
71. Hayes, *Misión de Guerra*, 273.
72. Wigg, *Churchill y Franco*, 225.
73. Martínez Nadal, *Antonio Torres*, 18.
74. Millás, "El quinto," 30–1.

References

Briggs, Asa. *The Golden Age of Wireless. Vol. 2 of the History of Broadcasting in the United Kingdom*. Oxford: Oxford University Press, 1995.

Briggs, Asa. *The War of Words. Vol. 3 of the History of Broadcasting in the United Kingdom*. Oxford: Oxford University Press, 1995.

Burns, Tom. *The Use of Memory: Publishing and Further Pursuits*. London: Sheed & Ward, 1993.

Burns Marañón, Jimmy. *Papá espía: Amor y traición en la España de los cuarenta* [Papa spy. Love, Faith, and Betrayal in Wartime Spain]. Barcelona: Debate, 2010.

Churchill, Sir Winston S. *Memorias. La Segunda Guerra Mundial: Su hora mejor* [The Second World War: Their Finest Hour]. Vol. 2. Barcelona: Plaza y Janés, 1965.

Cole, Robert. *Britain and the War of Words in Neutral Europe, 1939–45: The Art of Possible*. London: MacMillan Press, 1990.

Gillespie, Marie, and Alban Webb. "Corporate Cosmopolitism: Diasporas and Diplomacy at the BBC World Service, 1932–2012." In *Diasporas and Diplomacy: Cosmopolitan Contact Zones at the BBC World Service (1932–2012)*, edited by Marie Gillespie and Alban Webb, 1–21. London: Routledge, 2013.

Hayes, Carlton H. *Misión de guerra en España* [Wartime Mission in Spain]. Madrid: Epesa, 1946.

Hoare, Samuel. *Embajador ante Franco en misión especial* [Ambassador on Special Mission]. Madrid: Sedmay, 1977.

Martínez Nadal, Rafael. *Antonio Torres y la política española del Foreign Office (1940–1944)* [Antonio Torres and the Spanish Policy of Foreign Office 1940–1944]. Madrid: Casariego, 1989.

Millás, Jaime. "El quinto poder de la BBC [The Fifth Estate of the BBC]." *Triunfo* 759 (1977): 30–31.

Monferrer Catalán, Luis. *Odisea en Albión: Los republicanos españoles exiliados en Gran Bretaña* [Odyssey in Albion: The Spanish Republican Exiled in Great Britain]. Madrid: De la Torre, 2007.

Moradiellos, Enrique. *Franco frente a Churchill* [Franco vs. Churchill]. Barcelona: Peninsula, 2005.

Nicholas, Siân. *The Echo of War: Home Front Propaganda and the Wartime BBC, 1939–1945*. Manchester: Manchester University Press, 1996.

Rawnsley, Gary D. *Radio Diplomacy and Propaganda: The BBC and VOA in International Politics, 1956–1964*. London: McMillan Press, 1996.

Scannell, Paddy, and David Cardiff. *Social History of British Broadcasting: Serving the Nation, 1922–1939*. Oxford: Basil Blackwell, 1991.

Schlesinger, Philip. *Putting Reality Together: BBC News*. London: Routledge, 1992.

Schulze Schneider, Ingrid. "Éxitos y fracasos de la propaganda alemana en España: 1939–1944 [Successes and Failures of German Propaganda in Spain: 1939–1944]." *Mélanges de la Casa de Velázquez* 31, no. 3 (1995): 197–217.

Serrano Súñer, Ramón. *Entre Hendaya y Gibraltar* [Between Hendaya and Gibraltar]. Madrid: Epesa, 1947.

Stenton, Michael. *Radio London and Resistance in Occupied Europe: British Political Warfare, 1939–1943*. Oxford: Oxford University Press, 2000.

Townson, Nigel. *Palabras recobradas* [Recovered Words]. Madrid: Debate, 2000.

Wigg, Richard. *Churchill y Franco:La política británica de apaciguamiento y la supervivencia del régimen, 1940–1945* [Churchill and Franco: The British Policy of Appeasement and the Survival of the Regime, 1940–1945]. Barcelona: Debate, 2005.

OUR ENEMY'S ENEMY
Selling Britain to occupied France on the BBC French Service

Kay Chadwick

This article focuses on representations of Britain to occupied France by the BBC French Service via its flagship programme Les Français parlent aux Français *[The French speak to the French]. It first examines the establishment of the service and the formulation of a British propaganda strategy on occupied France. It then explores the service's efforts to foster French belief in Britain as France's friend and ally, and to rationalise key issues and incidents which challenged that narrative. Simultaneously, it positions French Service endeavours alongside the propaganda delivered on French national radio, known as Radio Vichy, in order to explore the exchanges about Britain between French propagandists who spoke on behalf of different Frances. In so doing, the article provides a close reading of the original French Service broadcasts which covers a larger corpus of material than has hitherto been documented in published collections, and which extends existing knowledge on the topic.*

Speaking on the BBC French Service on 3 August 1940, Pierre Bourdan, who would broadcast from London throughout Germany's Occupation of France, proclaimed to listeners back home: 'We are in England because England remains the enemy of Germany'.[1] On 26 August, his colleagues Jacques Brunius and Pierre Lefèvre declared in unison: 'I prefer to see the English in their country than the Germans in mine',[2] a slogan authored by Jean Oberlé, another French Service luminary, which thereafter regularly featured in the schedules.[3] Such words demonstrate the strength of feeling of those French who rejected the Armistice which France had signed with Germany on 22 June 1940, and who elected to continue to fight from Britain for an alternative France. Simultaneously, they symbolise a determination to counteract anti-British propaganda in France, which worked to capitalise on critical wartime events involving Britain within a sustained and bitter war of words with London for influence over opinion in France.[4]

This article investigates representations of Britain to occupied France on the BBC French Service. This subject arises only as a subsidiary question in research published to date on wartime broadcasting in French from London. The dominant strand of earlier work has been the powerful association between the French Service broadcasts and the wartime narrative of Free France and resistance, a theme sustained in popular memory by photographs of Charles de Gaulle speaking into a BBC microphone. Such images evoke 18 June 1940 when De Gaulle, recently arrived in London, broadcast his historic appeal to resistance to his compatriots back home, an important (but unrecorded)

This is an Open Access article distributed under the terms of the Creative Commons Attribution License (http://creativecommons.org/licenses/by/4.0/), which permits unrestricted use, distribution, and reproduction in any medium, provided the original work is properly cited.

moment in the story of Anglo-French broadcasting, even if few actually heard it at the time. Equally, they conjure up 22 June 1940, when De Gaulle broadcast again (this time recorded), calling on 'all Frenchmen who want to remain free to listen to my voice and follow me'.[5] In her detailed study of the history of French-language radio during the Second World War, Eck privileges analysis of the ways in which broadcasting from London contributed to the construction of the legend of Free France and to support for domestic resistance. The theme of 'voices of freedom' also marks Luneau's wide-ranging analysis of the work of Radio London (meaning the BBC French Service) between 1940 and 1944. Elsewhere, Stenton has studied Radio London and resistance in the context of British political warfare across occupied Europe, while Brooks has included the BBC French Service as one component within his study of the wider development and delivery of British propaganda to occupied France.[6]

By focusing on the portrayal of Britain by the French Service, this article sets out to extend such research, and so to offer a fuller understanding of the strategies of wartime radio propaganda in French. It first examines the establishment both of the service and of an official British propaganda strategy on occupied France. It then explores the French Service's efforts to foster French belief in Britain via its flagship programme *Les Français parlent aux Français* [The French speak to the French], analysing the strategies employed in broadcasts to profile notions of Britain as France's friend and ally, and to rationalise key issues and incidents which challenged that narrative. To that end, it is rooted in a close reading of the original French Service broadcasts, which covers a larger corpus of material than has been documented in the principal published collection, edited by Crémieux-Brilhac, where broadcasts profiling Britain are limited in number in an otherwise extensive anthology, and a wider period than in the more recent volumes published by Pessis, which are restricted in timeframe to the first two years of the Occupation.[7] At the same time, the article assesses the French Service broadcasts in the light of anti-British propaganda from France. This was an extensive operation delivered not only on radio but also via newsreels, films, brochures and newspapers, aspects of which have been examined by Passera, Chadwick and Jennings, but in relation only to single incidents, or to shorter timeframes or different media than here.[8] In aural propaganda, on which we will concentrate, Radio Paris and Radio Vichy were the main voices in the domestic broadcasting framework. The former, despite its French presenters, was under the direct control of the Germans and was consequently widely distrusted by the French listening public as the 'microphone of the occupier',[9] a reaction sustained by the French at the BBC with another of Oberlé's slogans, invented in September 1940: 'Radio Paris lies, Radio Paris lies, Radio Paris is German'.[10] This article therefore focuses predominantly on Franco-French exchanges, between French who spoke on behalf of different Frances, positioning BBC French Service endeavours alongside the propaganda delivered on French national radio, commonly known as Radio Vichy. Significant to its provision, as we shall see, was the period from 1942, when the arrival on Vichy airwaves of two subsequently high-profile speakers—Paul Creyssel and Philippe Henriot—marked the beginning of a combative broadcasting response to the French at the BBC.

Broadcasting to France: Provision, Policy and Practice

When France fell in June 1940, broadcasting in French at the BBC was still a fledgling service, dedicated mainly to the delivery of news bulletins in French. It had begun, unplanned, on 27 September 1938 when, at the government's request and in order to prevent mistranslation by foreign broadcasters, the BBC responded rapidly to world events by swiftly translating Neville Chamberlain's address to the nation on the deepening international crisis for immediate re-transmission in French, German and Italian.[11] Bulletins in French continued daily thereafter until war conferred a new importance on the service, bringing an increase in broadcasts and the expansion of the team (of, until then, just three announcers) with the recruitment of French nationals living in Britain alongside Britons fluent in French.[12] Correspondence received by the BBC from France indicates that, during the Phoney War, listeners turned to the BBC as a more reliable source of information than France's state-run radio *Radiodiffusion nationale* (RN), appreciating the BBC's provision of prompt and honest news, however disheartening its content, in contrast to what Vaillant terms 'banalities from a censored public network at home'.[13] In June 1940, and in response to the problems France faced in the delivery of news as her transmitters fell progressively into German hands, the BBC undertook to provide an 'authoritative news service by arrangement with the French government for the French people'.[14] Scheduled to begin on 17 June, this was delayed for technical reasons.[15] But, from 19 June, the day after De Gaulle's first appeal, six 15-minute bulletins were broadcast daily. The focal transmission was at 20:15, followed by a 15-minute 'entertainment called *Ici la France* [This is France]—a programme in French, for the French, by the French',[16] which incorporated the voices of RN staff in London.

Once France had signed the Armistice, RN correspondents in London were summoned home, and the French Service thereafter assumed a new character. Cecilia Reeves, the BBC's Senior Talks Assistant for the French Service, set out to put together a different type of programme 'which would not just be in French, but which would communicate French thought and aspirations'.[17] The daily news bulletins in French continued, but, in addition, *Ici la France* was doubled to 30 minutes from 30 June, and Michel Saint-Denis, the well-known theatre director who would operate at the BBC under the name Jacques Duchesne, was appointed to lead the project. The new programme was described by the BBC as 'the first truly national programme broadcast by the BBC to an occupied European country'[18]—a profile reinforced by its rebranding as *Les Français parlent aux Français* on 6 September 1940—and used news as a springboard for the delivery of commentaries on wartime events, issues and personalities. Broadcast every evening at 20:30, and preceded by 10 minutes of news and by a 5-minute slot entitled *Honneur et Patrie* (Honour and Homeland, which gave the official political viewpoint of Charles de Gaulle's 'Fighting France' movement), *Les Français parlent aux Français* would be at the heart of French Service programming for the next four years. It retained an almost exclusively French presence, one notable exception being Winston Churchill's stirring declaration (in French) of British determination and of solidarity with the French, broadcast on 21 October 1940 as Vichy headed towards collaboration with Germany.[19]

From the start of the war, all media output which might concern military security was subject to British censorship. More generally, French Service broadcasts were subject to British editorial supervision in the shape of Darsie Gillie, a keen Francophile who had become BBC French news editor in 1940, and who was well regarded by the French on the team.[20] No British governmental strategy for propaganda to German-occupied countries was in place in June 1940, so the BBC initially operated without official guidance, determining broadcast content itself. Brooks demonstrates that official strategy, when it did begin to take shape in September 1940, corresponded with BBC practice to date, indicating that the latter was well conceived.[21] Boosting French morale, restoring and maintaining belief in Britain (in terms of both her wartime and her post-war policy), fostering hatred of the Germans, and positioning Vichy as Germany's instrument were central objectives. These goals subsequently informed the French Service 'directives' produced by the Political Warfare Executive (PWE), which, from August 1941, was responsible for British propaganda strategy towards enemy and occupied nations.[22] At their heart lay the crucial message that what Britain was doing was in France's interests, since France's freedom depended upon a British victory. French Service broadcasts were officially subject to PWE directives, although it seems that their implementation rested on a negotiation around shared interests rather than on a requirement to execute British policy. A powerful card in the delivery of pro-British propaganda on the French Service lay in the fact that much of it was spoken by French nationals. However, they should not be thought of as puppets in British employ, although Henriot, their most infamous broadcasting rival in France, often defined them thus.[23] Notably, their BBC staff contracts included a 'conscience clause' according to which they could not be required to do anything they judged contrary to French interests.[24] But, more than this, and as agreed at a meeting on 3 October 1940 attended by Duchesne, Bourdan, Reeves and Gillie, while British interests necessarily influenced what could and could not be said, it was equally important that the French should represent their own national interests, having regard to French reception. Propaganda to France, it was concluded, must reflect a French attitude.[25]

This decision demonstrates a judicious grasp of the workings of propaganda. Studies of its theory and practice, such as Ellul's classic work, highlight that, for propaganda to have an impact, it has to have a receptive audience and be believed; moreover, to be fully effective, propaganda must connect with factual truth rather than with manifest falsehood.[26] On this basis, the French Service had to establish a bond with listeners. Broadcasts had to be based in truth, if they were not to lose credibility or be easily undermined by enemy propaganda, of which the team constantly had to take note. Consequently, they had to package high and low points realistically, neither over-selling military successes nor dwelling on losses suffered, respecting their task 'to inform, to communicate good news and bad'.[27] The French in London also had to show that they were in contact with and sensitive to what the French were feeling and experiencing under German occupation in France. They had to appeal to those able and willing to resist the Germans, but not offend those who were unwilling or unable. Further, broadcasts had to negotiate tricky waters when the positioning of Britain as France's ally sat uneasily in a context of potentially damaging events, such as British military action in parts of the French Empire or the RAF's bombing of strategic targets within France, or when political incidents cast doubt on British intentions and on what a British victory might mean for the future of France and French sovereignty. Hence, as the PWE directive for 12–26 July 1942 stressed, broadcasts had to take 'every opportunity of letting the French know as much as possible about the British people and their spirit and will in fighting this war'. But they also had to bear in mind that, in the prevailing circumstances, the French could be expected to take an interest in British actions and affairs 'only in so far as these affect the liberation of France, and France's own future'.[28]

Propaganda about Britain: First Endeavours

Throughout the Occupation, audiences in France were exposed to an anti-British propaganda omnipresent in printed and visual media.[29] Radio, then in its heyday, was no less a key medium for the communication of this message. The goal was to reactivate long-standing French suspicions of a perfidious Albion by asserting that Britain had again betrayed France, portraying the British as unfeeling killers of French, and feeding fears that Britain was seeking through this conflict to realise her enduring designs on the French Empire. Unsurprisingly, such propaganda capitalised obsessively on the British retreat at Dunkirk in June 1940 and Britain's strike on the French fleet at Mers el-Kébir on 3 July. On 11 July, Philippe Pétain, Vichy's Head of State, in one of his rare direct references to Britain in his speeches broadcast on Radio Vichy, alluded to both incidents when he accused Britain of first abandoning and then unjustifiably attacking France.[30] This speech came two days after Maurice Schumann in London had offered 'a defence of Franco-British friendship', asserting at the same time that Vichy had 'abandoned defending what remained of France, begged for the Armistice, and obtained it on the most humiliating terms', and now obeyed Germany in everything, including opposing Britain.[31] These two broadcasts thereby defined points of reference which opposing French voices would repeatedly mobilise in their subsequent propaganda about Britain.

An official document on British propaganda to France outlines that, in 1940:

> the first task of our radio propaganda to France was to counteract Anglophobia, to rebuild confidence in Britain's power to continue the war, and to expose the attempts made by the Germans to separate France from England to create divisions amongst the French people themselves.[32]

This approach was encapsulated in Duchesne's broadcast on 2 August, when, with a nod to Franco-British historical differences, he urged the French not to fall for current efforts to set France against Britain, and thereby betray 'the camp that fights for freedom'.[33] In this respect, striking the right note in propaganda terms was crucial in the aftermath of Dunkirk and Mers el-Kébir. With a view to inspiring French confidence in their neighbour, upbeat broadcasts offered a vision of an unconquered and resilient Britain which had the resources and the resolve to continue the fight against Germany alone. This came through especially strongly in the multiple broadcasts from August 1940 which extolled the RAF's achievements during the Battle of Britain, predictably downplayed in propaganda from France, or which profiled the stoicism of Londoners in their bombed but defiant city, or which stressed that, although Germany had enslaved Vichy, she could not overcome Britain.[34] But it was equally important not to alienate a defeated and demoralised France whose forces could justifiably be said to have suffered at British hands, and, to that end, much effort was spent on explaining British actions and attitude towards France. Following the line established by Schumann on 9 July, a core strategy employed was to associate France and Britain closely, insisting that, despite everything, Britain was France's friend, that she valued and respected France, was sympathetic to her position, and had no ambitions other than to see her liberated and restored to her former standing. On 25 July, Eve Curie reassured the French 'You are not alone!' and affirmed Britain as 'the only great European country still free and strong, the only country to continue to stand as guarantor of France's future'. These facts about Britain mattered, she concluded, not sentiment.[35] She continued the assault on 6 August, rubbishing the notion that Britain had betrayed France at Dunkirk, while, on 28 October, a refugee soldier insisted that Britain bore France no animosity over the Armistice.[36]

Significantly, this set of broadcasts focused on people as well as nation, giving a human face to Britain which endeavoured to establish France and Britain as connected communities of ordinary citizens facing corresponding ordeals, and with shared hopes and goals. Hence, the trials of life in wartime Britain and the sterling work of Britons for the war effort juxtaposed recognition of the difficulties of life in defeated France and respect for French endurance of adversity.[37] Broadcasts spoke of the British welcome given to French refugees, countering propaganda from France that the British were preventing the return home of French soldiers stranded in Britain after Dunkirk.[38] Or they highlighted positive views of Britain from French in France, as detailed in letters received by the BBC, the content of which was broadcast back home.[39] Radio Vichy and Radio Paris claimed the letters were invented or exaggerated, but Reeves and Oberlé both confirm their authenticity, the latter emphasising that their moving tone could never have been fabricated.[40]

In parallel, negative positioning of Vichy's association with Germany was employed to frame positively the alliance between Britain and Free France, drawing a portrait (which would be sustained throughout the Occupation) of Free France as Britain's partner and Vichy France as Germany's subordinate. While Radio Vichy classified London as the bastion of dissident French, and Pétain on 13 August alluded to the French at the BBC as 'false friends' and so 'true enemies', they in turn asserted 'Vichy is not France!'.[41] Curie's broadcast on 25 July had also neatly distinguished between 'the French people', defining Britain as their ally, and 'the France of capitulation', meaning Vichy France.[42] Such declarations simultaneously dissociated ordinary French from Vichy and invited them to locate the true France in Free France, physically outside France in Britain but present via the airwaves. Britain and France may sometimes have been divided, the French team acknowledged, but 'London is now the bastion of unoccupied France'.[43] Furthermore, collaboration—which Pétain announced to the French on Radio Vichy on 30 October 1940 after his meeting with Hitler at Montoire on 24 October[44]—was defined as nothing short of 'handing France over to the enemy'.[45] The argument repeated by London was that the enemy had no interest in France other than as a resource, and that France's pain was Vichy's fault. Focus rested on the 400 million francs which France had to pay Germany daily under the Armistice.[46] Moreover, it was frequently alleged that Germany was asset-stripping metropolitan France, and, unlike Britain, intended to prey on her Empire.[47]

Intense as it was, the success of Vichy's anti-British propaganda campaign in the second half of 1940 seems to have been limited. Official reports for Vichy on the situation in the occupied zone, compiled from monitored postal and telephonic communications, and from intelligence supplied by different Vichy ministries, indicate that, from August 1940, public opinion was turning increasingly in Britain's favour such that, by October, most French in the occupied zone desired a British victory.[48] Interestingly, the report dated 16 October posits that the majority held this view more out of growing hostility towards Germany than actual Anglophilia, thereby illustrating the logic of the theory of 'our enemy's enemy'. But it also judged the populations of Normandy and Brittany to be 'in the avant-garde of Anglophilia', welcoming recent British air incursions over their coastlines, and it noted that Parisians were freely commenting on 'British radio' in public, causing concern in official circles. This suggests that two things were being positively noticed by the French, at least in the occupied zone: continued British military action, and the BBC French Service broadcasts. Certainly, neither Vichy nor Germany discounted the BBC's efforts. It cannot be known for certain how many French across France listened to the BBC during the Occupation, although Vichy's reports refer generally to sizeable and increasing audiences from October 1940.[49] Correspondingly, Oberlé notes that the team knew by May 1941 that they were listened to across France, based on information from Free French intelligence services, on the letters the BBC received, and on what those recently arrived from France told them.[50] Of course, listening in itself is no indicator of the development of pro-British sentiment, since listeners may simply have wanted more accurate and faster news than Radio Vichy was judged to supply, qualities which Vichy intelligence noted that the French widely ascribed especially to the BBC.[51] But listening is a prerequisite for impact, and both Germany and Vichy feared the BBC's potential influence, as their actions reveal. In fact, Germany banned listening to the BBC in the occupied zone as early as 30 June 1940. Vichy followed suit on 28 October, when it banned listening in public in the unoccupied zone to the BBC or any other 'anti-national' station, then extending this a year later to listening to the BBC in private.[52] Both introduced penalties of varying severity for non-compliance, although these seem to have been unevenly applied, if at all,[53] and the French listened nonetheless. No doubt aware of this, Radio Vichy and Radio Paris each determinedly attacked the French Service, which naturally saw their manoeuvres 'as clear evidence that our team in London has huge influence in France'.[54]

Argument and Counter-argument from 1941

Promotion of Franco-British friendship and alliance, and of Britain's war effort, remained a consistently weighty part of French Service provision from 1941. Many such broadcasts were predictable in their positive content and confident tone, employing the classic propaganda methodology of message repetition to reinforce their upbeat reading of Britain. One set focused on the French who chose to be in Britain, intended to boost morale back home with the message that France was still fighting through these French, who were upholding French honour. Hence, broadcasts frequently featured French nationals who had recently arrived in London to join the battle for liberation, or portrayed French military personnel in training at bases across Britain, operating with loaned British equipment.[55] In addition, three weekly series are of note. From 3 January 1941, *Courrier de France* [Letters from France] formalised the earlier sporadic use of pro-Britain correspondence from France.[56] This ended in February 1943, after Germany had occupied all of France the previous November and moved to prevent correspondence reaching Britain. *Courrier d'Angleterre* [Letters from Britain] appeared in its place from 3 March 1943.[57]

Ostensibly written by Britons to French friends, the letters were designed to profile daily life in Britain and to emphasise a line of long-standing Franco-British friendship. Unsurprisingly, Radio Vichy and Radio Paris disputed the authenticity of these letters, as they had those the BBC received from France. Reeves and Nina Epton (another British BBC employee), who had both lived in France, contributed letters,[58] suggesting that at least some were possibly addressed to real friends. But it is highly likely that they were intended for a wider audience and written to a brief, since the content gels closely with PWE objectives. Simultaneously, multiple broadcasts continued to record energetic civilian and military activity across Britain. Many of these appeared from March 1943 in a third series, *Chronique d'Angleterre* [News from Britain], celebrating, for example, women's work in the Land Army, or the Royal Marines, or portraying a nation of resilient Britons well-prepared for the long haul.[59]

Such positive profiling of Britain was solid but fundamentally easy propaganda which did not directly engage the French Service with opposing voices. It was thus comparable in approach to Vichy's promotion to the French of its programme of National Revolution or of Pétain himself. More challenging for the French Service to handle were issues and incidents beyond but involving Britain, on which enemy propagandists had seemingly credible things to say to a traumatised people anxious about their own existence and their nation's current and future status. These resulted in 'connected' propaganda which rested on argument and counter-argument, suggesting that each side considered it important to tackle what the other was saying, and to do so swiftly at especially critical moments. The substance and tone of these exchanges were crucial, since what was at stake was emotional identification with the French people, potentially a powerful factor in the struggle for influence over public opinion on the issues or parties involved. One recurring theme was the integrity of the French Empire. This had featured in exchanges in 1940, when Pétain had broadcast on Radio Vichy on 30 October that collaboration would ensure 'French unity', and the French in London had replied on 1 November that collaboration would bring demands from Germany that would chip away at the 'intact French Empire'.[60] The argument was resurrected from May 1941, when Vichy allowed Germany to use air bases in the French mandate of Syria. The French Service pounced on the opportunity to attack Vichy's propaganda that Britain had designs on French territory, arguing that this incident proved that Germany, not Britain, was the real threat.[61] But this was disputed by Admiral Darlan, then Pétain's second-in-command, speaking on Radio Vichy on 23 May, prior to a lengthy and strident statement on 31 May in which he outlined the 'negatives' of 20 years of Franco-British relations.[62]

The subsequent British-led Allied campaign in Syria and Lebanon, which began on 8 June and was intended to prevent Germany from using the mandates as a springboard to attack Allied-held Egypt, gave Vichy propagandists an easy opening to charge Britain again with expansionist ambitions. But it also raised the sensitive and thus potentially trickier issue of Britain fighting against French forces loyal to Vichy. Both sides instantly undertook to speak in emotive terms to the French in France and in the Levant, each accusing the other of killing French nationals. The French Service positioned British and Free French forces as combat partners in Syria, entreated Vichy's troops not to fire on their compatriots, and reignited questions about Vichy's status vis-à-vis Germany by reflecting on 'the extent to which Vichy will have succeeded in spilling French blood on behalf of

Germany'.[63] Pétain's counter-statement the same day criticised the Free French forces who, 'supported by Britain's imperial forces, do not hesitate to spill the blood of their brothers who are defending the unity of the Empire'.[64] A Vichy communiqué dated 11 June, and widely reported in the media, retaliated further, labelling Britain the 'aggressor', fiercely resisted by troops who had sacrificed themselves for the true France.[65] But, as claims flew back and forth over the summer, French opinion seems to have found Vichy's argumentation less credible, since prefects reported that the majority of French considered Germany, not Britain, to be the primary cause of all problems.[66]

Despite the USA's entry into the war in December 1941, Vichy's propagandists reserved a special venom for Britain, the old enemy who incarnated the wider Anglo-Saxon world. The war of words about British action in the French Empire intensified from May 1942 with Britain's campaign to take Vichy-controlled Madagascar in order to prevent Japan taking it as a base. On 7 May, as the port of Diego Suarez surrendered to the British just two days after their invasion, the French in London broadcast that Madagascar remained French.[67] That evening on Radio Vichy, Creyssel, who had been named Vichy's Director of Propaganda Services in April, strove to press Anglophobic buttons, soberly warning that British promises to restore Madagascar to France could not be relied upon, given Britain's historical practice elsewhere.[68] Henriot, who had broadcast weekly since February unconstrained by a formal government brief, was rather more dramatic in his appraisal, as was his wont. In three consecutive broadcasts from 16 May, he lambasted the British as 'highwaymen', declared that Madagascar was another Syria and Mers el-Kébir, and made doom-laden predictions about British intentions for North Africa.[69] When Britain intensified operations in mid-September, Henriot continued his onslaught, describing Madagascar on 19 September as 'fresh prey for British thieves', then railing on 3 October against its 'abduction'.[70] The French Service commented in restrained terms, explaining on 22 October that the total occupation of Madagascar was essential to protect Allied communications.[71] It subsequently made much of the end of hostilities and of the handover of Madagascar to Free French authority to emphasise the island's return to 'normality', and the message that Britain had no expansionist goals.[72] Jennings suggests that Vichy's printed propaganda on British intentions for Madagascar was counter-productive because it wearied audiences who had heard the same laboured arguments time and again since Mers el-Kébir.[73] In all likelihood, audiences felt much the same about Vichy's radio propaganda, which peddled the same message. In terms of impact, the majority of prefects in the free zone reported in May 1942 that public opinion seemed instead to trust Anglo-American reassurances on Madagascar, while in September they commented that the renewed fighting had prompted no notable reaction in their regions.[74] This is not to say that the French were indifferent to the fate of their Empire. But, quite naturally in a time of domestic crisis, they were more likely to be engaged by incidents closer to home, within or affecting metropolitan France, events on which the rival propaganda machines would play hard.

In this respect, from 1942, argument raged especially over the Allied bombing of France. For the purposes of bolstering confidence in Britain, it was important that RAF action was positively profiled, as we saw earlier in the French Service's representation of the Battle of Britain. But this became problematic when civilian deaths occurred. For example, when the RAF bombed the Renault factory in Boulogne-Billancourt, near Paris, on 3 March 1942, the French Service swiftly and repeatedly stressed the strategic nature of the target (which produced lorries for Germany), justifying the action in the interests of destroying the German war machine. But they were also careful to express regret for the heavy casualties among Renault's French workforce, and to depict them as the innocent victims of German policy to compel France to work for the occupier.[75] Predictably, enemy propaganda held that Britain bombed indiscriminately and did not care for the consequences. For Henriot, a master of melodrama and scaremongering, Britain had simply progressed from killing French soldiers to assassinating innocent civilians. On 7 March, he sarcastically took issue with British promises to help France and contended that Britain had no excuse for bombing French factories while German ones remained operational.[76] It was a powerful argument for a suffering population, intended to shake confidence in British operations. That same day, Schumann worked a similarly emotive line, describing the Renault workers as victims of Germany in the same way as Gabriel Péri, a prominent French communist and resister shot by the occupier in December 1941. All were heroes who had died for France, Schumann proclaimed, and the whole nation was in mourning.[77]

In March 1942, propaganda from Britain seemed the more influential, for it was reported by prefects in the occupied zone that, while deploring civilian deaths, most French there accepted the explanations given by British radio and regarded such incidents as the inevitable consequence of Germany's exploitation of French factories.[78] From London, broadcasts thereafter nurtured this reading, encouraging the French to set the bombings in the wider context of the war and striving to communicate that French safety was a central British concern. As Bourdan declared on 2 June 1942: 'The French judge and understand; they know that British air forces are accomplishing a sad duty in France'.[79] Moreover, much airtime was given to broadcasting British Government warnings, intended to avoid as far as possible 'the spilling of French blood during our operations'.[80] Nonetheless, for the French team in London, the Allied bombings were 'our nightmare' and an issue on which Henriot was a weighty adversary.[81] On 7 March 1943, for example, Henriot recalled Boulogne-Billancourt, labelling the British 'harvesters of coffins'.[82] On 27 March, from London, Oberlé employed similar 'anniversary' tactics, reminding listeners of the positive reaction of locals to the successful RAF attack on Saint Nazaire on 28 March 1942.[83] When the raids intensified in September and October 1943, Creyssel talked of 'acts of piracy', whereas Henriot spoke more forcefully of a British attack on French civilisation.[84] Then, in spring 1944, at the height of the bombings, Henriot evoked the whole of France as a cemetery, offering a terrifying vision of the price of liberation intended to alarm. A series of heated exchanges ensued. On 30 April, Boivin described the bombings as a tragic necessity.[85] Henriot retaliated on 6 May, accusing the French team of shameless hypocrisy. Bourdan hit back that evening, lamenting the civilian victims of the bombings, but alleging that Henriot regretted there were not still more.[86] In return, on 26 May Henriot denounced his rivals in London, pointing out that they were safe abroad, unlike the majority of French people.[87] The French team agonised over how to engage with Henriot on the bombings, for, theatrical as he was, his words were based in truth and they knew that his argumentation could appeal to those who had suffered directly.[88] Indeed, in spring 1944, prefects across France reported that opinion was turning against the Allies due to the intensification of the bombings, and they credited Henriot with reducing Anglophilia if not Germanophobia, a conclusion corroborated by Free French agents active in France.[89]

Handling Allied military failures posed further challenges for the French in London, for these offered enemy propagandists an opening to allege incompetence, and denying the truth would have made the French Service look untrustworthy. The disastrous landing at Dieppe in August 1942, for example, resulted in 4098 Allied casualties and prisoners (in contrast to 591 German) and caused much disappointment in France. But French Service broadcasts did not dwell on the losses. Rather, they tried to focus attention on an upbeat if somewhat thin argument, which held that the landing of Allied troops weakened Germany's claim that the coastline of occupied Europe was invulnerable. More convincingly, they located Dieppe within the wider war, promising that it '[was] not the main attack, but [was] one step closer to it'.[90] But, in propaganda terms, Dieppe was more valuable to their rivals. On 20 August, Creyssel emphasised that the raid was ill-prepared and he flagged the predominance of Canadian troops as a way of accusing Britain of shielding her own.[91] Two days later, Henriot mocked more sharply the 'landing turned re-embarkation' as the Allies fled.[92] In reply, the French team attempted a more optimistic counter-narrative, concluding 'We will be back, and one day, fear not, it will be for good', before again pitching Dieppe as a preparatory exercise for a main landing.[93] However, no doubt with the management of French expectations in mind, no hint of a timeframe was proposed. When the Allies did successfully land in North Africa on 7–8 November 1942, Oberlé profited to contest Vichy's repetitive propaganda that the British were 'lamentable' and the Americans would 'never be ready'.[94] The response was predictable. On 12 November, Creyssel decried the 'occupation of our Africa by the Anglo-Saxons', while, two days later, Henriot talked emotively of 'the savage amputation of part of our Empire'.[95] Prefects in both zones noted that the landing in North Africa once more raised French hopes of an end to the war, but that morale soon dipped again, not least because of the subsequent total Occupation of France by Germany.[96]

One controversial incident in North Africa gave Vichy propagandists the opportunity to foster doubts about Allied attitudes towards the status of Free France. This revolved around Vichy's Admiral Darlan, who was in Algiers when the Allies landed and who 'converted' to become Head of French North Africa, with Allied recognition but in the face of Free French opposition. For the Allies, Darlan was a temporary expedient, recruited to secure swift French cooperation in North Africa. But, for the Free French, Darlan could be nothing but a traitor to the real France, despite his conversion. On 21 November 1942, De Gaulle's 'Fighting France' acolytes declared they could no longer speak on the BBC, since this would suggest acceptance of the Darlan deal. Duchesne's BBC team joined the walkout on 3 December, once Darlan's position had been formalised,[97] not returning until after Darlan's assassination on Christmas Eve,[98] which brought a sudden close to an otherwise seemingly insoluble issue. From a longer-term perspective, the incident demonstrates the limitations of the idea of 'our enemy's enemy' when pragmatism collides with patriotism in a sensitive context. For Henriot, speaking on 27 December, in the wake of Darlan's death, it was yet more proof that any French affiliated with the Allies were mere 'bit players, extras, puppets'.[99]

The future status of France was an equally delicate issue, given her wartime position as a defeated nation. Sensitivities heightened as the post-war period increasingly became the focus. On 14 July 1943, Anthony Eden, British Foreign Secretary, spoke on the French Service of the importance of 'the restoration of France to her full sovereignty and to her natural place among the great powers of the world'.[100] But, on 25 November 1943, Jan Smuts, the South African Premier who had been co-opted to the British war cabinet, gave a speech in which he articulated the post-war disappearance of France as a great power. The PWE was concerned that the situation could seriously lower morale and shake French confidence in Allied intentions towards France.[101] This appreciation manifestly lay behind the French Service's explanation of events, broadcast between 5 and 9 December 1943, where realism was tempered with efforts to reassure. For as long as Germany remained a military threat, it said, political questions were ancillary. But the restoration of France as a great power was of primary importance to Britain, as Churchill had frequently said, and many in Britain disagreed with Smuts.[102] The situation was nonetheless powerful fuel to Vichy propaganda that Britain intended post-war France to be a satellite, secondary nation, as trumpeted by Henriot on 13 December 1943.[103] As the PWE had feared, and despite the reassurances offered from Britain, Smuts' speech caused indignation in France, and pro-British sentiment dipped as a result.[104]

Conclusion

The French Service's broadcasts strove hard, as we have seen, to explain and justify British action and policy, and to reinforce the message that the French could have confidence in Britain, both in time of war and in respect of the future. The reports on public opinion in both zones during the Occupation prepared by prefects for Vichy, alongside intelligence reports prepared for the Free French authorities, indicate that support for Britain in France did fall when the Allied camp suffered losses, as at Dieppe, whenever the RAF bombed France, but especially in spring 1944 in advance of the Normandy landing, and when issues related to France's future seemed to cast doubt on British intentions. However, the reports equally demonstrate that support for Britain grew overall throughout the war.[105] Correspondence received from France by the BBC is divided between those French who felt positively about Britain and those who were more sceptical.[106] But most seemed to accept that Britain was a necessary ally, and hoped for an eventual British victory. The scale of anti-British propaganda in France during the Occupation is a measure of the support Vichy and Germany believed Britain to have, support which was undoubtedly reinforced by the work of the BBC French Service. On radio, Vichy's propagandists worked hard to demonise the British, none more so than Henriot, whose rhetorical skill drew large audiences appreciative of his sparring with the French at the BBC, especially once he was Vichy's top propaganda man from January 1944. But, in the end, even Henriot failed to convince, for few agreed with what he said.[107] Battering the British would never get the French to like the Germans. For Britain was, after all, if not a textbook friend, at least still the enemy's enemy.

Notes

1. Institut d'Histoire du Temps Présent (hereafter IHTP), BBC French Scripts, June 1940–September 1944, B50-B101 (B52), 3 August 1940. Subsequent shortened references to this archive take the form (for example) IHTP-B52, 3 August 1940. Transcripts of the BBC French Service broadcasts may also be consulted at the BBC Written Archives Centre, Caversham (hereafter BBC-WAC). All translations from French are my own.
2. IHTP-B52, 26 August 1940.

3. Oberlé, *Jean Oberlé vous parle*, 50.

4. The French Service broadcasts generally use the terms 'Angleterre' [England] and 'Anglais' [English], although they are normally referring more widely to Britain and the British. Such usage remains common practice in France. When quoting in translation from the broadcasts, this article generally uses 'Britain' or 'Briton' to reflect their actual wider focus.

5. The French texts of De Gaulle's broadcasts are available at: http://www.charles-de-gaulle.org/pages/l-homme/dossiers-thematiques/1940-1944-la-seconde-guerre-mondiale/l-appel-du-18-juin.php. Accessed July 21, 2014.

6. Eck, *La Guerre des ondes*; Luneau, *Radio Londres*; Stenton, *Radio London*; and Brooks, *British Propaganda to France*.

7. Crémieux-Brilhac, *Les Voix de la liberté*; and Pessis, *Les Français parlent aux Français*.

8. Passera, 'La propagande anti-britannique'; Chadwick, 'Across the Waves'; and Jennings, "'Angleterre, que veux-tu à Madagascar'".

9. Eck, *La Guerre des ondes*, 53.

10. Oberlé, *Jean Oberlé vous parle*, 50.

11. BBC, *Voici la BBC*, 7.

12. Ibid., 24–5. The surviving schedules are held at the BBC-WAC in non-catalogued, chronological sequence. For details of the Service's French and British personnel, see BBC-WAC, French Service Staff Lists, 1939–1945 (no reference number).

13. Vaillant, 'Occupied Listeners,' 153. Eck, *La Guerre des ondes*, 64–5, makes the same point. For letters received by the BBC, see BBC-WAC, E1/704. 200 of the more than 1000 letters in this file dated between 1940 and 1944 are published in Luneau, *Je vous écris de France*.

14. 'Bulletins for the French.' *The Times*, June 21, 1940.

15. BBC, *Voici la BBC*, 29.

16. 'Bulletins for the French.' *The Times*, June 21, 1940.

17. BBC, *Voici la BBC*, 31. See also Reeves's unpublished memoir, BBC-WAC, 550/1.

18. BBC, *Voici la BBC*, 35.

19. IHTP-B54, 21 October 1940.

20. Oberlé, *Jean Oberlé vous parle*, 156–63.

21. Brooks, *British Propaganda to France*, 66–70, 104–5.

22. For the surviving directives, see BBC-WAC, E1/702/1, and Archives Nationales, Paris (hereafter AN), F/1a/3726.

23. See, for example, his broadcast 'Les menteurs salariés' ['The salaried liars'], 13 June 1942, in Henriot, *Ici Radio France*, 38–9.

24. Eck, *La Guerre des ondes*, 62.

25. 'Minutes,' 3 October 1940. British Library, London (hereafter BL), MS81143.

26. Ellul, *Propagandes*, 259–302.

27. IHTP-B61, 28 May 1941.

28. BBC-WAC, E1/702/1.

29. Passera, 'La propagande anti-britannique,' 130–6.

30. Pétain, *Paroles aux Français*, 55–6.

31. IHTP-B51, 9 July 1940.

32. 'British Propaganda to France,' n.d., BL, MS81143. Although undated, the document's content indicates that it was written after Pétain's famous speech of 12 August 1941, in which he spoke of an 'ill wind' across France (Pétain, *Paroles aux Français*, 136–48).

33. IHTP-B52, 2 August 1940. The French Service broadcasts cited hereafter are representative but not isolated examples of the themes discussed.
34. IHTP-B52, 14 August 1940; IHTP-B55, 7 November 1940; and IHTP-B53, 28 September 1940.
35. IHTP-B51, 25 July 1940.
36. IHTP-B52, 6 August 1940; and IHTP-B54, 28 October 1940.
37. IHTP-B51, 31 July 1940; and IHTP-B55, 13 November 1940.
38. IHTP-B55, 18 November 1940.
39. IHTP-B53, 7 September 1940.
40. BBC-WAC, 550/1, 28–9; Oberlé, *Jean Oberlé vous parle*, 151.
41. Pétain, *Paroles aux Français*, 60; and IHTP-B55, 19 November 1940.
42. IHTP-B51, 25 July 1940.
43. IHTP-B56, 31 December 1940.
44. Pétain, *Paroles aux Français*, 89–91.
45. IHTP-B55, 3 November 1940.
46. IHTP-B53, 24 September 1940.
47. IHTP-B55, 23 November 1940; IHTP-B56, 18 December 1940.
48. IHTP, *Synthèses*. See especially the 1940 reports dated 2 and 29 August, 4 and 16 October, 17 November.
49. Ousby, *Occupation*, 237, notes that Vichy statistics indicate that some three million radios in France were tuned to the BBC by the beginning of 1942. This is a plausible figure, but no source is given for the claim, and Vichy's own official reports consulted give no such figure.
50. Oberlé, *Jean Oberlé vous parle*, 110.
51. IHTP, *Synthèses*. See, for example, the reports dated May 1941 and November 1942.
52. Brooks, *British Propaganda to France*, 119–22.
53. Eck, *La Guerre des ondes*, 57.
54. IHTP-B55, 14 November 1940.
55. IHTP-B58, 27 February 1941; IHTP-B73, 12 May 1942.
56. IHTP-B57, 3 January 1941.
57. IHTP-B83, 3 March 1943.
58. IHTP-B86, 9 June 1943; IHTP-B87, 28 July 1943.
59. IHTP-B83, 26 March 1943; IHTP-B84, 30 April 1943; and IHTP-B86, 9 June 1943.
60. Pétain, *Paroles aux Français*, 90; and IHTP-B55, 1 November 1940.
61. IHTP-B61, 19 May 1941.
62. 'L'allocution radiodiffusée de l'Amiral Darlan'; and 'L'Angleterre veut détruire la France'.
63. IHTP-B62, 8 June 1941.
64. Pétain, *Paroles aux Français*, 118.
65. See, for example, *Journal des débats politiques et littéraires*, 13 June 1941.
66. Laborie, *L'Opinion française sous Vichy*, 252.
67. IHTP-B73, 7 May 1942.
68. AN, F/41/306, 'Madagascar,' 7 May 1942. The surviving texts of Creyssel's broadcasts are held in this file and in AN, F/1a/3795, Ministère de l'Intérieur, Écoutes radiophoniques, 1943. Selected broadcasts are published in Creyssel, *Passion et mission de la France*.
69. Henriot, *Ici Radio France*, 30–5.

70. Ibid., 66–9.
71. IHTP-B78, 22 October 1942.
72. IHTP-B80, 20 December 1942.
73. Jennings, "'Angleterre, que veux-tu à Madagascar,'" passim.
74. IHTP, *Synthèses*, May 1942 and September 1942.
75. IHTP-B71, 4–6 March 1942.
76. Henriot, *Ici Radio France*, 9–10.
77. IHTP-B71, 7 March 1942.
78. IHTP, *Synthèses*, March 1942.
79. IHTP-B74, 2 June 1942.
80. IHTP-B77, 23 September 1942.
81. Oberlé, *Jean Oberlé vous parle*, 168, 211.
82. Henriot, *Et s'ils débarquaient?*, 283–5.
83. IHTP-B83, 27 March 1943.
84. Creyssel, *Passion et mission de la France*, 205–8; and Henriot, *Et s'ils débarquaient?*, 387–90, 399–402.
85. IHTP-B96, 30 April 1944.
86. IHTP-B97, 6 May 1944.
87. Chadwick, 'Across the Waves,' 345–7. For the texts of Henriot's 1944 broadcasts, see Chadwick, *Philippe Henriot: The Last Act of Vichy*.
88. Oberlé, *Jean Oberlé vous parle*, 216.
89. IHTP, *Synthèses*, April 1944, May 1944; and AN, AG/3(2)/395, 'Le danger de la propagande de Philippe Henriot,' 31 March 1944.
90. IHTP-B76, 19 August 1942.
91. Creyssel, *Passion et mission de la France*, 55–7.
92. Henriot, *Ici Radio France*, 58–9.
93. IHTP-B76, 22 August 1942; 27 August 1942.
94. IHTP-B79, 8 November 1942.
95. Creyssel, *Passion et mission de la France*, 91–5; Henriot, *Ici Radio France*, 80–1.
96. IHTP, *Synthèses*, November 1942; December 1942.
97. Crémieux-Brilhac, *Les Voix de la liberté*, I, xxiv.
98. Eck, *La Guerre des ondes*, 109.
99. Henriot, *Ici Radio France*, 103.
100. IHTP-B87, 14 July 1943.
101. BBC-WAC, E1/702/1, Directive dated 29 November–5 December 1943.
102. IHTP-B92, 5–9 December 1943.
103. Institut National de l'Audiovisuel, Paris. Archives politiques: éditoriaux de Philippe Henriot, 'Le Maréchal Smuts a fait un discours tapageur,' 13 December 1943.
104. IHTP, *Synthèses*, December 1943.
105. IHTP, *Synthèses*; AN, F/1a/3743, Opinion publique; and AN, F/1a/3744, État d'esprit: contrôle postal.
106. BBC-WAC, E1/704; and Luneau, *Je vous écris de France*.
107. Chadwick, 'Across the Waves,' 349–50.

References

"Allocution radiodiffusée de l'Amiral Darlan [Radio Broadcast by Admiral Darlan]." *Journal des débats politiques et littéraires*, May 24, 1941.

"L'Angleterre veut détruire la France déclare, à Paris, l'Amiral Darlan [Britain Wants to Destroy France, States Admiral Darlan in Paris]." *Le Matin*, June 1, 1941.

Archives Nationales, Paris. AG/3(2)/395. Bureau central de renseignements et d'action [Central Bureau of Intelligence and Operations].

Archives Nationales, Paris. F/1a/3726. Political Warfare Executive. Directives pour les services français de la BBC, juin 1942–septembre 1944 [Directives for BBC French Service, June 1942–September 1944].

Archives Nationales, Paris. F/1a/3743. Opinion publique [Public Opinion].

Archives Nationales, Paris. F/1a/3744. État d'esprit: contrôle postal [State of Mind: Correspondence Monitoring].

Archives Nationales, Paris. F/1a/3795. Ministère de l'Intérieur. Écoutes radiophoniques, 1943 [Ministry of the Interior. Radio Monitoring, 1943].

Archives Nationales, Paris. F/41/306. Service de la Propagande [Propaganda Services].

BBC. *Voici la BBC* [This is the BBC]. London: BBC, 1944.

BBC Written Archives Centre, Caversham. 550/1. Cecilia Reeves Gillie. History of the BBC Wartime French Service (1977).

BBC Written Archives Centre, Caversham. E1/702/1. Policy/PWE Directives for BBC French Service, August 1941–March 1944.

BBC Written Archives Centre, Caversham. E1/704. France/French Service/Listener Correspondence (1939–1945).

BBC Written Archives Centre, Caversham. French Service Staff Lists, 1939–1945 (no archival reference number).

British Library, London. Michel Saint-Denis archive. MS81143. Vol. LIII. Propaganda and political aspects of broadcasts (1940–1944).

Brooks, Tim. *British Propaganda to France, 1940–1944: Machinery, Method and Message*. Edinburgh: Edinburgh University Press, 2007.

"Bulletins for the French." *The Times*, June 21, 1940.

Chadwick, Kay. "Across the Waves: Philippe Henriot's Radio War with the Free French at the BBC." *French Historical Studies* 34, no. 2 (2011): 327–355.

Chadwick, Kay. *Philippe Henriot: The Last Act of Vichy: Radio Broadcasts, January—June 1944*. Liverpool Online Series: Critical Editions of French Texts, 17 (2011). Accessed July 21, 2014. http://www.liv.ac.uk/cultures-languages-and-area-studies/french/liverpool-online-series/.

Crémieux-Brilhac, Jean-Louis, ed. *Les Voix de la liberté: Ici Londres, 1940–1944* [The Voices of Freedom: This is London, 1940–1944]. 5 vols. Paris: La Documentation française, 1975–1976.

Creyssel, Paul. *Passion et mission de la France* [France's Passion, France's Mission]. Paris: n.p., 1944.

Eck, Hélène. *La Guerre des ondes. Histoire des radios de langues françaises pendant la Deuxième Guerre mondiale* [The Battle of the Airwaves. A History of French-language Radio during the Second World War]. Paris: Armand Colin, 1985.

Ellul, Jacques. *Propagandes* [Propaganda]. Paris: Armand Colin, 1962.

Henriot, Philippe. *Ici Radio France* [This is Radio France]. Paris: Les Éditions de France, 1943.

Henriot, Philippe. *Et s'ils débarquaient* [What if They Landed]? Paris: Éditions Inter-France, 1944.

Institut d'Histoire du Temps Présent, Paris. B50-B101. BBC French Scripts, June 1940–September 1944.

Institut d'Histoire du Temps Présent, Paris. "Synthèses des rapports de préfets, 1940–1944 [Summaries of Prefects' Reports, 1940–1944]." http://www.ihtp.cnrs.fr/prefets.

Institut National de l'Audiovisuel, Paris. Archives politiques: éditoriaux de Philippe Henriot (no archival reference number).

Jennings, Eric. "'Angleterre, que veux-tu à Madagascar, terre française?' La propagande vichyiste, l'opinion publique et l'attaque anglaise sur Madagascar en 1942 [Britain, What Do You Want with the French Territory of Madagascar?' Vichy Propaganda, Public Opinion and the British Attack on Madagascar in 1942]." *Guerres mondiales et conflits contemporains* 246, no. 2 (2012): 23–39.

Laborie, Pierre. *L'Opinion française sous Vichy* [French Opinion under Vichy]. Paris: Seuil, 1990.

Luneau, Aurélie. *Radio Londres, 1940–1944. Les Voix de la liberté* [Radio London, 1940–1944. The Voices of Freedom]. Paris: Perrin, 2005.

Luneau, Aurélie. *Je vous écris de France: lettres inédites à la BBC* [I Write to You from France: Unpublished Letters to the BBC]. Paris: L'Iconoclaste, 2014.

Oberlé, Jean. *Jean Oberlé vous parle. Souvenirs de cinq années à Londres* [Jean Oberlé Speaks to You. Memories of Five Years in London]. Paris: La Jeune Parque, 1945.

Ousby, Ian. *Occupation: The Ordeal of France*. London: Random House, 1999.

Passera, Françoise. "La propagande anti-britannique en France pendant l'Occupation [Anti-British Propaganda in France during the Occupation]." *Revue LISA* 6, no. 1 (2008): 124–150.

Pessis, Jacques, ed. *Les Français parlent aux Français* [The French Speak to the French]. 2 vols. Paris: Omnibus, [2010] 2011.

Pétain, Philippe. *Paroles aux Français* [Words to the French]. Paris: Lardanchet, 1941.

Stenton, Michael. *Radio London and Resistance in Occupied Europe: British Political Warfare 1939–1943*. Oxford: Oxford University Press, 2000.

Vaillant, Derek. "Occupied Listeners: The Legacies of Interwar Radio for France during World War II." Chap. 6 in *Sound in the Age of Mechanical Reproduction*, edited by David Suisman and Susan Strasser, 141–178. Philadelphia: University of Pennsylvania Press, 2009.

REPATRIATED GERMANS AND 'BRITISH SPIRIT'
The transfer of public service broadcasting to northern post-war Germany (1945–1950)

Hans-Ulrich Wagner

Following the end of the Second World War, the ideals of public service broadcasting that had first been exemplified by the BBC came to lay the groundwork for a new type of broadcasting system in Northern Germany. This led to intensive discussions between British Military Officers and their German counterparts about the principles of public service broadcasting. Repatriated Germans came to play a crucial role. Having worked for the BBC German Service during their years of exile, some of them helped to nurture a new generation of democratic journalists. Focusing on these men, this article reveals the difficulties in transferring and adapting public service ideals. Making use of a wide range of sources, we highlight the multifaceted roles of the repatriated Germans, as both intermediaries and transmitters of public service broadcasting. We show how many of them came to play a pivotal role in resisting pressure from conservative forces in West German society.

Introduction

The BBC has been widely considered a role model for public service broadcasting in media history. This reputation was solidified when, in 1927, the British Broadcasting Company was repositioned as the British Broadcasting Corporation (BBC) having been granted the first Royal Charter in 1927.[1] The ideals of public service broadcasting were resolutely promoted by John Reith, its first Director General.[2] From its start in the late 1920s, the BBC had earned itself a first-rate reputation and took over an 'influential role', which was 'unparalleled elsewhere in the world'.[3] Aspirations were high: programmes aimed to inform, educate and entertain, while BBC staff were called on to serve British society as a whole.[4] This helped to promote the BBC's 'image of solidity', yet also resulted in some 'stolidity'.[5] Financed by a licence fee, the BBC declared itself independent from government rule, a decision which helped to shape an image of public service at its best and one that helped to cultivate the 'myth' of the BBC.[6] This paper takes this 'myth' as a point of departure, as we turn our attention to the transference of the public service ideal to post-war Germany. A variety of studies have also revealed how politically entangled the BBC was during this time.[7] Recent publications have drawn attention to the ways in which the BBC also used propaganda during the wartime, both at the 'Home Front'[8] and within their Foreign-Language Services. This also includes the German Service, following its inauguration in 1938 at the height of the Munich crisis.[9] But, despite its control by the Political Warfare Executive (PWE),[10] the German Service itself successfully perpetuated its image as a 'voice of truth' ('Stimme der Wahrheit') in publications of the German Service, that celebrated its anniversaries.[11] In 2003, a volume on the history of the BBC German Service took this slogan of 'Stimme der Wahrheit' as a title.[12]

Consequently, this ideal of public service was very much in favour when the Western Allied Military Governments set off to restructure a new and efficient broadcasting system in post-war Germany. This system was intended to serve the aims of demilitarisation and democratisation. Private-run and commercial radio stations dominated the US-American landscape, but these would not work in a conquered and ruined country. In addition, any structures that were seen to be too closely connected to the government would be firmly rejected. The German tradition of broadcasting had just provided important examples of how the media could be used in a potentially harmful way: Goebbels and his 'Reich Ministry of Public Enlightenment and Propaganda' had revealed the possible dangers of media, when they were directly controlled by a totalitarian regime. Years before, the broadcasting system in the Weimar Republic had become more and more part of state bureaucracy, finally collapsing because of increasing governmental influences.[13] As a result, British and US-American plans to use the media in occupied Germany ranged from the short-term policy of how to get suitable German employees to the long-term policy of building a broadcasting system that could never be used as an instrument of governmental control.[14]

There is a wealth of research on broadcasting in the British Occupation Zone[15] and on German emigrants coming back to occupied Germany.[16] Recognising the significance of this previous work, this paper looks more closely at concrete conceptions of refusal and rejection, in an attempt to deal with the difficulties faced by the British and Germans, as they endeavoured to transfer and adapt the ideals of public service broadcasting in the British Occupation Zone. In doing so, the focus is on German emigrants, who had fled to the UK during the Nazi era and who had worked for the BBC, especially for the BBC German Service during the war. As repatriated Germans in the British Occupation Zone, they worked for broadcasting stations of the Nordwestdeutscher Rundfunk and played an instrumental role as intermediaries and transmitters of knowledge about public service broadcasting.

Recruiting New Personnel

In the UK, there was a tremendous lack of detailed knowledge of how to deal practically with occupied Germany. Only a few internal memoranda had acknowledged this issue during wartime.[17] The existing files of the Control Commission for Germany/ British Element (CCG/BE) reveal that the British Warfare Executive had no clear mandate.[18] Sefton Delmer who played a decisive role in the set-up of German News Service and the Deutscher Presse-Dienst[19] reported that there was a great need for qualified personnel, following a visiting tour through the British Occupation Zone on 13 July 1945.[20] In various meetings in London, there was an agreement about the lack of British supervisors 'of high quality' and the need to train staff.[21] And it was here that these first returnees arrived. They consisted of a small number of men and only a handful of women, who had returned alongside Allied troops in the immediate aftermath of the Second World War.[22] The British and US military services had hired these volunteers. During the war, they had been trained to take over special tasks in occupied Germany.

In the British Zone, the CCG/BE was in charge of all political and societal affairs. It was a highly complex system of units and branches, meant to control all matters of public affairs, not least the media and especially the broadcasting stations.[23] As British-American cooperation in psychological warfare came to an end, the British founded the Public Relations/Information Services Control Group (PR/ISC), which was headed by Major General W.H. Alexander Bishop, the former Deputy Director of the PWE.[24] The media were controlled by the Information Control Units, while the Broadcasting Control Unit (BCU) was a sub-unit and took care of all broadcasting questions. One of them was the takeover of the existing broadcasting stations in Hamburg and in Cologne. Within a very short time, the station in Hamburg began transmitting on 4 May 1945, as 'Radio Hamburg. A Station of the Allied Military Government'. When the Cologne station started in September 1945, the broadcaster in the British Zone was called 'Nordwestdeutscher Rundfunk' (NWDR; Northwest German broadcaster).

In the immediate weeks following the war, no more than 100 people in total worked at the NWDR, which was later reduced to approximately 30 people in mid-1946. It was here that military and administration experts met radio professionals and saw the British working together with people of German descent. Among these were returnees like Walter Albert Eberstadt (1921–2014) and Alexander Maaß (1902–1971) who attempted to solve the shortage of adequate or qualified personnel.

Eberstadt was the son of a Jewish banker who grew up in Hamburg and escaped Nazi Germany in 1936. In 1940, this young German Jewish émigré joined the British Army and adopted the name Walter Everitt. He was trained as an officer, specialised in psychological warfare, and attended some courses at the BBC. In May 1945, the 24-year-old returned to his hometown Hamburg, wearing a British uniform with the rank of a major, tasked with the job of building up an efficient radio station in Hamburg. Eberstadt/Everitt later reflected on this time in his autobiography, writing that:

> I engaged the people who interested me in discussions and debates, I'd give them a meal, whisky, cigarettes or pipe tobacco and have them talk, talk, talk. If I concluded they were fundamentally decent, I was not put off by some affiliation with the old system.[25]

Eberstadt used an unconventional approach when he started to recruit new members of staff. He opted to screen potential candidates through one-to-one interviews, resulting in a hire-and-fire policy, where a single officer was given the authority to make staffing decisions. Due to the fact that their instructions were kept rather vague, Eberstadt could make the decision independently and gave his applicants a chance to prove themselves. The most famous example was Peter von Zahn. This young Wehrmacht officer and spokesman of a prisoner-of-war camp won over Eberstadt with the promise of democratic ideals. After Eberstadt had considered von Zahn to be 'okay', he on an impressive journalistic career. Peter von Zahn would later become one of the leading journalists in West Germany. His reports became popular and his comments could be regarded as significant democratic parables.[26] Increasingly, we can see that seemingly antagonistic 'parties'—Control Officers on the one hand, and German journalists on the other hand—came to consider themselves more and more as partners. This particular collaboration resulted in a lifelong friendship between Walter Albert Eberstadt and Peter von Zahn.[27]

Alexander Maaß pursued an altogether different strategy. As 'Production Chief', he was responsible for a range of different tasks, including the recruitment process.[28] As a former announcer and journalist at the Cologne radio station during the later years of the Weimar Republic, Maaß was an experienced practitioner and became a consummate networker at the NWDR. As a member of the German Communist Party in 1926, Maaß was also a political intellectual. In late 1931, he took some time off to travel to Moscow and help to build up the Soviet broadcasting station. In 1935, his exile had led him from Moscow to Spain, where he had worked for the Spanish Republican Radio and the 'Deutscher Freiheitssender 29,8'. It was in Spain that he was severely wounded while fighting for the Republicans. After escaping to France, he ended up in London in January 1942, where he started to work at the so-called 'black' radio stations (i.e. secret British radio stations purporting to be run by Germans).[29]

In June 1945, he came to Hamburg as a Civilian Officer of the BCU. He was assiduous, ambitious and aware of his own influence. He also believed that it was essential to discover where his former colleagues had ended up. This led to the exchange of correspondence between himself and his former associates. From these letters, we can see how Maaß set himself the goal of finding the 'right' personnel.[30] An in-depth analysis of the correspondence between Alexander Maaß and Ernst Hardt, his former boss at the Cologne station (dated from November 1945 to January 1947), reveals how differently Maaß judged his former colleagues.[31] By examining these messages, we can see that Maaß surprisingly did not pay attention to the role he himself had played during his time in exile, instead he chose to remain rather silent about his own past. Neither did he speak much about his political role in Moscow and the Spanish Civil War, nor about the various secret radio stations, where he had been working apart from the BBC German Service. Maaß' refusal to acknowledge his previous affiliations, together with the lack of knowledge about his political motivations, meant that he was often faced with the prospect of dealing with disparaging rumours about his past.

Training a New Generation—The NWDR-'Rundfunkschule' (Training School)

In January 1947, Hugh Carleton Greene, the Chief Controller of all broadcasting affairs in the British Zone, established a Training School at the NWDR in Hamburg. It was one of his first activities, after he had taken over the new position in the British Zone and had introduced himself to his new German employees: 'I have come to leave as soon as possible'.[32]

A 'Rundfunkschule' (Training School) of this kind was something new in German broadcasting history. There had been no German tradition in training radio journalists besides from 'learning by doing' in the Weimar Republic and some competitions for reporters and announcers during the 'Third Reich'. Consequently, the Hamburg 'Rundfunkschule' had to look at its predecessors from the BBC as an example of best practice. Before the war, three centralised training organisations had been founded at the BBC: 'a general Broadcasting school, a Secretarial school, and an Engineering school'.[33] Now, the

German counterpart was given the task to educate new journalists, similar to the BBC pre-war 'Broadcasting school' and to the BBC 'Resettlement training' from late summer of 1945.[34] The aim of the 'Rundfunkschule' was to recruit new journalistic talent and help them develop their skills. Moreover, the trainee programme was to reflect the general purpose of journalism and teach the students about their responsibilities as journalists in a democratic society.[35]

Openings for the training programme were publicly advertised and received applications from many eager candidates.[36] Greene had initiated the Training School and was the mastermind behind it, while the daily business was to be conducted by Maaß. Greene handed over all the organisational work to Maaß, as well as the recruitment of new talent.[37] Between January 1947 and July 1948, they ran three courses for up-and-coming young journalists. Documents reveal how teachers and practitioners had trained 55 men and 21 women in Hamburg. Within the following decades, many of these 76 went on to become the 'Who's Who' of West German journalism.

It was rare that Maaß took an active part in teaching a newer kind of independent and investigative journalism. Instead, his main job was to create possibilities for 'discussions'. At this time, most tutors were German journalists who already worked for the NWDR and only a few lecturers came over from Britain—out of 148 instructors, only 15 were British citizens. Former students recall how a particularly British way of thinking was taught at the school. Gerd Ruge (*1928), for instance, who later went on to become one of the most famous West German correspondents, remembers how 'calm' and 'reserved' the BBC-inspired style of production taught at the NWDR Training School appeared, especially compared to the 'propaganda frenzy of the Nazi broadcasting'.[38] We can see how Britons and Germans came together—from former practitioners at the BBC to German editors—to foster successfully a sense of 'British spirit'.[39]

Political Resistance to Public Service Broadcasting

The recruitment and training of German journalists was one way that knowledge about public service broadcasting was transferred during this time. Another aspect dealt with the adaptation and rejection of public service ideals. It turned out that the most powerful opponents were, in fact, the German parties.

Soon after the end of the war, British authorities allowed for the creation of German political parties. In 1946, the first elections took place in the new founded states ('Länder') of the British Occupation Zone. CCG/BE officers corresponded a great deal with German politicians about the media and broadcasting. On 31 January 1946, a first meeting of party representatives took place at the NWDR. The Political Division of CCG/BE, German politicians and NWDR employees discussed the possibility of giving five parties the chance to voice themselves in the election campaigns in March 1946.[40] A letter from one of the officers at the Political Division addressed to all 'gentlemen' (dated 4 February 1946) offered help about speaking in front of a microphone. It also clearly addressed the political responsibility expected of them during this time. It was recommended that speakers 'be constructive and not to spend your time in attacking other parties'.[41] It became clear that this kind of political mentoring was deemed necessary because many of the politicians were not used to these sorts of democratic conventions.

Soon after the first elections, German party members often complained about British personnel policies and the perceived neglect of German interests. One of these parties was the Social Democratic Party. Many of its members had spent their years of exile in London, notably Fritz Heine (1904–2002), who had escaped via Prague and Lisbon to London in 1941. He returned to North Germany in February 1946 and went on to become one of the key figures in the party executive of the SPD.[42] Being one of the influential media professionals in the SPD directorate, Fritz Heine at once claimed the responsibility of modernising the traditional party newspapers. He was also accountable for broadcasting matters. Heine turned to Allan Flanders, officer in the German Political Division, to thank him for the invitations to broadcast round-table talks, but Heine was also unhappy that all parties would be granted the same amount of time on air: 'We, therefore, desire that at these round-table talks the parties should be represented to their strength as expressed in the recent elections'.[43] The German Political Division of CCG/BE was far from being amused about demands like this and rejected his request.

It very soon became clear that German party politicians were to play a very decisive role within the organisation of this new system of broadcasting. Hans Bredow (1879–1959), for instance, warned Greene about the threat of the German parties.[44] Bredow had been one of the most influential personalities in early German broadcasting history. As a high-ranking officer in the Post Ministry, he had established many of the rules for German broadcasters during the 1920s. According to him, broadcasting was considered to be an instrument of culture and education, and therefore meant to be controlled by the states ('Länder'), not by the central government. After the Second World War, Bredow worked as a consultant for the US-American occupation authorities but was also in contact with the British authorities, especially with Greene.

The British, however, tried to remain consistent in their approach. In a memo from November 1946 entitled 'The future of Broadcasting in the British Zone'[45], the following recommendations were made: first, that the broadcasting system in the British Occupation Zone should not be built up according to the borders of the states: Schleswig-Holstein, Niedersachsen, Nordrhein-Westfalen and Hansestadt Hamburg. Instead, it was intended to be organised as one centralised system for the whole British Zone—a characteristic that marked a major difference in the organisation of broadcasting stations in the US-American Zone.[46] Second, that this memo also stated that the British authorities intended to stay in charge and oversee the nomination of future board members.

To Ensure the 'NWDR-Statut'

However, the CCG/BE did not succeed after all. The public service broadcasting system that was brought into being by law on 31 December 1947—the so-called 'NWDR-Statut'—reveals that compromises were made.[47] In the months before, Hugh Greene had led in-depth talks with representatives of the churches, the parties, the trade unions, the universities, etc.[48] But, in the long run, the political resistance to the public service model was successful to some degree. In the Zonal Advisory Council ('Zonenbeirat'), Greene faced the demands of CDU, SPD, FDP, KPD and DP, and had to come to terms with them. Between 15 August 1947 and 12 November 1947, in the first four meetings of the subcommittee, the 'Rundfunkbeirat des Kulturpolitischen Ausschusses' (Broadcasting

Advisory Board of the Committee for Cultural Policy), Greene had to compromise in the end, especially concerning the delegations of party representatives to the new boards. In the fourth meeting, it was decided that one of the boards, the 'Hauptausschuss' ('Principal Committee'), should consist of 16 members, among them state politicians, the four prime ministers and four representatives of Educational Interests, mandated by the four state governments in the British Zone.[49] This 'Hauptausschuss' had the right to elect the seven members of the 'Verwaltungsrat' ('Administration Board'), which could appoint the Director General.

But such transference and adaptation of a checks-and-balances system of public service broadcasting in post-war Germany faced one core problem. Whereas in Great Britain the members of the 'Board of Governors' were appointed by the Crown, there was no sovereign institution in Germany. Therefore, the 'Hauptausschuss' was supposed to be a cross-section of relevant societal representatives. But the representatives did not only come from associations such as the 'German Federation of Journalists' or the 'Federation of German Theatres'. As already stated, at least half of the members were state politicians.

Greene considered this strong political influence as a compromise which he had to subscribe to. Repeatedly and publicly, he criticised the influence political parties had. Instead, Greene and the British officers pledged their allegiance to independent broadcasting.[50] But the German politicians did not welcome even this new element of public service broadcasting in Germany. A closer look at contemporary sources of the post-war period reveals a certain amount of resistance against this model. Public service broadcasting was considered to be something that British occupation forces had imposed. It was not described as a 'gift' but publicly attacked as a 'hard nut to crack' by no less a figure than Konrad Adenauer, the first Chancellor of the Federal Republic of Germany.[51] And even Fritz Heine continued his harsh criticism. The Social Democrats argued that all principles supposedly above party lines would only lead to 'political uncertainty and non-transparency'. They could not approve any authority which was not bound to 'true democratic control' but instead inclined to support 'corporative' and 'non-transparent lobbying'. The SPD considered the societally relevant representatives—suggested by members of the 'Hauptausschuss' from the Catholic Church, the Protestant Churches, the trade unions, etc.—to be 'political non-transparent persons' and wanted them to be counteracted by 'politicians without any mask'. All these quotations are taken from a memorandum on the constitution of the NWDR, which was published in 1948.[52]

In order to deal successfully with this type of political pressure, Greene became the NWDR's first Director General. Instead of choosing to appoint a German colleague, Greene took over responsibility for the institute between 1 January 1948 and 15 August 1948. During this time, he installed two additional returnees from London in leading positions.

The first one was Walter D. Schultz (1910–1964), who had worked for the BBC German Service from 1941 to 1945. In May 1948, Greene offered him a position designed especially for him: the NWDR 'Außenreferat' (Department of Foreign Affairs). In doing so, Greene gave Schultz a great deal of power. It was one of Greene's last decisions before he retired and went back to London. This 'Außenreferat' combined a series of different tasks and responsibilities.[53] Above all, Schultz had to keep contact with political parties. Schultz, a member of the SPD himself, built bridges for party representatives and integrated them into daily broadcasting. In 1949, he started the radio show 'Political Forum', a series of political talks to promote democratic ways of opinion making. Schultz also was the mastermind behind Adolf Grimme, the first German Director General of the NWDR, elected on 15 August 1948. Whenever Grimme defended journalistic freedom, Schultz was the man behind the scene, for example, when Peter von Zahn was attacked by ministers of the CDU and by the Chancellor, Konrad Adenauer, due to critical comments.[54]

The second leading associate was Albin Stuebs (1900–1977). Stuebs was a writer, who had escaped via Prague to London in 1938. After having been discharged from custody as an 'enemy alien' in December 1941, he had started to work for the BBC 'workers' programme'. As a returnee, Stuebs came back to Germany early in October 1947 and worked at the broadcasting station in Hamburg.[55] From April to July 1948, Stuebs gave lectures on the 'organization of the BBC' in the third course of the Training School, introducing journalistic principles to the participants. But after this third course, Stuebs— along with Maaß—reorganised the Training School. From 1948 onwards, it was no longer used as an actual school but changed into a department designated to explain the assignments and activities of public serving broadcasting to the public. Until 1955, a number of classes were given for societally important groups, such as teachers, students, writers, farmers, clergymen, etc. In doing so, the NWDR Training School was explicitly regarded as a 'bridge between broadcasting and the public'[56] and can be understood as an intermediary institution designed to explain public service broadcasting.

First Practical Tests for the Public Service Broadcaster NWDR in 1948/1949

Between the time when the NWDR was set up as a public service station on 31 December 1947, and until Hugh Greene retired as Director General on 15 August 1948, heavy rumours spread about the new broadcasting system in North Germany. They were caused by provocative broadcasts, occasional controversial financial transactions, but mostly related to questions of personnel policy. Party-political arguments played a crucial role in public debates, due to the fact that (1) Adolf Grimme became Director General, while also a member of the SPD and former minister of education and cultural affairs in Lower Saxony and (2) that the Chairman of the 'Verwaltungsrat' was firstly Heinrich Georg Raskop and later on Emil Dovifat, who were both members of the CDU. Every decision that was approved by the Director General caused an immediate reaction by the Chairman and vice versa.

Some of the repatriated Germans found themselves at the centre of these debates. The former emigrants became the objects of smear campaigns. Press articles reported how conservative politicians had been keeping dossiers on 'left-wing'-NWDR employees.[57] One of these dossiers has been preserved, an anonymous communique on 'political, actual and economic deficits at the NWDR'.[58] In this file from December 1949, former emigrants including Maaß, Schultz and Stuebs were accused of being committed communists. The 16-page dossier focused mainly on their seemingly suspicious work abroad during the Nazi years. They also made the following notes about Walter D. Schultz:

> Schultz is said to be the head of the communist group at the NWDR (...). Apparently, he plays a double game, as he works for the Secret Service and is on friendly terms with the

Social Democrats Dr. Kurt Schumacher and Fritz Heine, but at the same time supports communism. (author's translation)[59]

Based on dossiers like this, the conservative press published a number of articles. Under the headline 'NWDR' the 'Hamburger Allgemeine Zeitung' told its readership on 19 November 1949 that this station was 'a nest eroded by termites' (author's translation), and that a lot of former communists worked in leading positions. For the CDU-run newspaper it was obvious: the NWDR was a political instrument dating back to 1933. Journalists working for the conservative press saw themselves as fighters for a broadcasting station as a 'true institution of the people', one that was supposed to be 'really German' and 'the real Hamburg type' (author's translation).[60] This source was chosen because it caused reactions at the NWDR. The NWDR forced the chief editor to reveal the name of the employees who had been defamed in such a way. Those mentioned included Maaß, Stuebs and Schultz, among others.[61] Shortly afterwards, the SPD-run newspaper 'Hamburger Echo' complained about the 'evil of these offences' (author's translation) and claimed connections to the broadcasting policy of Raskop as Chairman of the 'Verwaltungsrat' as well as to the inauguration of Konrad Adenauer as first CDU Chancellor.[62] These press articles are examples taken from an extensive amount of available information. By studying these debates, it became clear that in its early years the NWDR was widely considered to have been at the centre of a 'broadcasting crisis' and a 'house of great intrigues' (author's translation).[63]

Conclusions

British officers carefully monitored all these arguments at the NWDR. After all, they were also suspicious about communist endeavours. 'We are keeping a watchful eye on developments in NWDR and in particular on the possibility of the emergence of an anti-occupational trend', the Deputy Chief of ISD wrote to the Deputy Regional Commissioner of Hamburg on 17 June 1949.[64] He and the officers of the British Military Government recognised all too clearly that the establishment of the NWDR as a public service broadcasting station by law at the end of 1947 was only the first step. So they eagerly watched how this broadcasting station worked and whether its staff were able to contribute to the new democracy. Facing the rumours caused by Grimme's personnel policy during the first half of 1949, the Deputy Chief of ISD expressed his hopes that all the aggression against the NWDR in the public sphere would not eliminate the 'British spirit'.[65]

In conclusion, it was this 'British spirit' that was established after the end of the Second World War with the strong support of a small number of former exiles.

First, this 'spirit' was transferred to experienced journalists who were given the chance to work at the broadcasting stations in the British Zone and to a lot of young Germans who were trained at the Training School or who started their job 'learning by doing'. The men and women who referred to this 'British spirit' in their work as broadcasting employees became intermediaries and transmitters in the sense of 'political actors'.[66] They also became defenders of a democratic political system and of a media system fighting for its non-governmental independence.

Second, the development of broadcasting in Germany became closely linked with the ideals of public service. Although established as a compromise compared to British

REVISITING TRANSNATIONAL BROADCASTING

ideals, the institutional framework of the NWDR served as a blueprint for Germany's public broadcasting system. This legacy had to meet with scepticism and disapproval. It had to prove its practicability and value. It was a learning process of how to deal with the new public broadcasting system, not only, but especially for the relevant societal representatives of the 'Principal Committee' (Hauptausschuss) respectively later on of the 'Broadcasting Board' (Rundfunkrat). Our analysis of documents has revealed evidence of strong governmental and party-political influence between 1947 and 1950. There was still much to be debated, negotiated and decided upon during the 1950s. Many of these setbacks and stories (some still waiting to be told) can be used to highlight the complex history of the German media during this time. But by the end of the 1950s and during the early 1960s it became quite clear that for the first time West German journalists successfully established what Christina von Hodenberg calls a 'critical public sphere' (2006)[67]. When the Norddeutscher Rundfunk (NDR), successor of the NWDR, celebrated its 50th anniversary in 2006, Wolfgang Hoffmann-Riem, a former Federal Constitutional Court Judge, put it similarly[68]: the German public service system laid down in the immediate post-war years by the NWDR can be considered both a challenge and a success in the long run.

Notes

1. Briggs, *The Birth of Broadcasting*, 325ff.; Scannell and Cardiff, "Public Service Broadcasting".
2. Reith, "Introduction".
3. Chignell, *BBC handbooks*.
4. Scannell and Cardiff, "Public Service Broadcasting"; Hilmes, *Network Nations*, 47–62.
5. Nicholas, *The Echo of War*, 4.
6. Ibid., 1.
7. For example, Briggs, *Sound and Vision*.
8. Briggs, *The War of Words*; Nicholas, *The echo of war*; Baade, *Victory through Harmony*.
9. Dove, "Introduction", X.
10. Richter, *Political Warfare Executive*.
11. For example, BBC External Services, *'Hier ist England' – 'Live aus London'*.
12. Brinson and Dove, *'Stimme der Wahrheit'*. Despite the popular slogan quoted in the title of the volume, the editor declares in his introduction: 'Wartime broadcasts by the BBC were a crucial contribution to the British war effort' (Dove, "Introduction", X).
13. Concerning German broadcasting history between 1924 and 1932, see Leonhard, Joachim-Felix, ed., Programmgeschichte des Hörfunks in der Weimarer Republik, München: Deutsche Taschenbuchverlag, 1997; concerning especially Goebbels and broadcasting in the 'Third Reich' see: Mühlenfeld, Daniel. "Joseph Goebbels und die Grundlagen der NS-Rundfunkpolitik." *Zeitschrift für Geschichtswissenschaft* 54, no. 5 (2006): 442–467.
14. Kutsch, "Unter britischer Kontrolle", 85–96; Clemens, *Britische Kulturpolitik in Deutschland 1945–1949*.
15. Tracey, *Das unerreichbare Wunschbild*; Goergen, "Der britische Einfluß"; Roelle, "Der britische Einfluß"; Kutsch, "Unter britischer Kontrolle"; Brüning, "Die BBC als Vorbild"; Wagner, "Das Ringen um einen neuen Rundfunk".

REVISITING TRANSNATIONAL BROADCASTING

16. Biller, *Exilstationen*; Krohn and von zur Mühlen, *Rückkehr und Aufbau nach 1945*; Wagner, *Rückkehr in die Fremde?*; Clemens, "Remigranten in der Kultur- und Medienpolitik der Britischen Zone"; Wagner, "Über alle Hindernisse hinweg".

17. How the CCG/BE dealt with the lack during the first months revealed the files in: The National Archives (TNA), Public Record Office (PRO), Foreign Office (FO) 898/401.

18. Bruce Lockhart to Secretary of State, 23 February, 1945. TNA, PRO, FO 898/401; see also Richter, *Political Warfare Executive*, 378ff.

19. Bayer, *How deas is Hitler?*; Eumann, *Der Deutsche Presse-Dienst.*

20. "By contrast to the American, the arrangements in the British Zone are still woefully incomplete (…). I urged Brigadier Neville to consider making Hamburg the basic centre of a prototype news service both for radio and newspaper", quotations from: Delmer, Sefton. Report. 1 June, 1945. TNA, PRO, FO 898/401.

21. So the report on a meeting at Bush House, 3 September 1945. TNA, PRO, FO 898/401. This need was also expressed in various reports and letters of officers between May and December 1945. TNA, PRO, FO 1050/791; 1056/25; 1056/26.

22. Leighton-Langer, *X steht für unbekannt.*

23. Birke et al., *Akten der britischen Militärregierung in Deutschland.*

24. Richter, *Political Warfare Executive*, 403.

25. Eberstadt, *Whence We Came, Where We Went*, 333.

26. Jacobmeyer, "Politischer Kommentar und Rundfunkpolitik".

27. Telephone interview of the author with Walter Albert Eberstadt, 2003; Walter Albert Eberstadt. [obituary for Peter von Zahn], 6 August, 2001. Research Center Media History, Hamburg (subsequently cited as RCMH).

28. Telephone directory of the NWDR. Effective July 1946. RCMH; Press releases of the NWDR 1945–1947. RCMH. The best way to study Maaß' strategy derives from a corpus of correspondence, 15 letters from Alexander Maaß to Ernst Hardt as well as 16 letters from Ernst Hardt to Alexander Maaß. These letters have been preserved at the Deutsches Literaturarchiv (DLA) in Marbach am Neckar. Quotations follow the original documents. The correspondence was published by Mira Đorđević (Đorđević, "Pioniere des deutschen Rundfunks"). Wagner's study of so-called 'first letters' is based on this correspondence (Wagner, "Wir müssen hart bleiben").

29. Pütter, *Rundfunk gegen das "Dritte Reich".*

30. Alexander Maaß to Ernst Hardt, 14 December, 1945. DLA. Literary remains Ernst Hardt.

31. Alexander Maaß to Ernst Hardt, 14 November, 1945. Ibid.

32. Greene, *Entscheidung und Verantwortung*, 46–47 (author's translation).

33. Harding, "The Past and Future of Staff Training", 29.

34. Ibid., 32.

35. Schwarzkopf, *Ausbildung und Vertrauensbildung.*

36. [Press releases] "Eine Rundfunkschule des NWDR." Die Ansage, Mitteilungen des NWDR, 22–28 December, 1946: 1; "Ab 20. Januar Rundfunkschule." Die Ansage, Mitteilungen des NWDR, 29 December, 1946–4 January, 1947: 4. The applications have been preserved in the Staatsarchiv Hamburg (StA HH), 621-1/144. 191 and 192. Within the research project on the NWDR, a study on the 'Training School' was undertaken by Dietrich Schwarzkopf (*Ausbildung und Vertrauensbildung*).

37. Archival sources on the NWDR "Training School" have been preserved at the StA HH, 621-1/ 144, 191, 192, 229.
38. Ruge, *Unterwegs: Politische Erinnerungen*, 49 (author's translation).
39. A series of interviews with alumni of the 'Rundfunkschule' were conducted at the RCMH between 2001 and 2007. Hildegard Stallmach, Gerd Ruge, Hans Joachim Werbke, Helga Boddin, Wolfgang Jäger and Hans Scholz referred to the BBC, when they remembered discussions about democratic principles and the societal role of journalists at the 'Training School'.
40. PR/ISC Group to Political Division, February, 7th, 1946. TNA, PRO, FO 1049/498.
41. Lt.Col. N.G. Annan, Political Division, 'an alle Gentlemen', 4 February, 1946. TNA, PRO, FO 1049/498.
42. Appelius, *Heine*.
43. TNA, PRO, FO 1049/502.
44. Deutsches Rundfunkarchiv. Frankfurt/Main. A 15. Hans-Bredow-Archiv.
45. Memorandum of 30 November, 1946. TNA, PRO, FO 1049, 502.
46. In the US-American Zone, each parliament of the states Hessen, Bavaria, and Württemberg-Baden had to pass a law on a public service broadcasting system widely according to the NWDR-'Statut'. See e.g. Rasack, "Parteieneinfluß und Rundfunkaufsicht".
47. Amtsblatt der Militärregierung Deutschland. Britisches Kontrollgebiet, No. 22, 656–660.
48. "Correspondence Hugh Carleton Greene." Westdeutscher Rundfunk (WDR) Köln. Historical Archive (HA), 4264.
49. Bundesarchiv Koblenz. Z 2. Zonenbeirat. 1946–1949. See Quellen zur Geschichte des Parlamentarismus und der politischen Parteien. Vierte Reihe: Deutschland seit 1945. Band 9/I. Düsseldorf: Droste Verlag 1993–94.
50. [Press release] "Ueberreichung des NWDR-Statuts." Die Ansage, Mitteilungen des NWDR, 30 December, 1948; Greene's speech on 30 December, 1948, has been preserved at the Norddeutscher Rundfunk, Sound Archive; Greene, "Anfänge des NWDR".
51. Konrad Adenauer on a public rally on 21 May, 1950. Sound document. Westdeutscher Rundfunk, Sound Archive (quotes translated by author).
52. Sozialdemokratische Partei Deutschlands, *Denkschrift über Verfassung und Programmgestaltung des NWDR* (author's translation).
53. In memoriam Walter D. Schultz (August 1964) [obituaries]. Norddeutscher Rundfunk, Department "Recherche, Presse und Buch".
54. Jacobmeyer, "Politischer Kommentar und Rundfunkpolitik", 378–383.
55. Wallace, "'Lob der Emigration': Albin Stuebs".
56. Stuebs, "Was ist 'Rundfunkschule'?", 75 (author's translation).
57. See e.g. "Platonisch interessiert." Der Spiegel, 26 January, 1950, 5–6.
58. WDR, HA, 9509.
59. Ibid.
60. "NWDR." Hamburger Allgemeine Zeitung, 18 November, 1949. The author is anonymous; chief editor of the newspaper at this time was Hans-Georg von Studnitz, a former high-ranked employee of Goebbels' ministry; see: Asmussen, Nils. "Hans-Georg von Studnitz. Ein konservativer Journalist im Dritten Reich und in der Bundesrepublik." *Vierteljahreshefte für Zeitgeschichte* 45 no. 1 (1997): 75–119.

61. Copies of the correspondence between NWDR and the 'Hamburger Allgemeine Zeitung' have been filed by the office of the Chairman of 'Verwaltungsrat', Emil Dovifat. RCMH.
62. "CDU-Treibereien um den NWDR. 'Spanienkämpfer' als politische Belastung." Hamburger Echo, 28 November, 1949.
63. Von Lojewski, Werner. "Führungskrise. Eine Rundfunkkrise als Symptom unserer Zeit." Frankfurter Allgemeine Zeitung, 6 February, 1950; Marein, Josef. "Das Haus der großen Intrigen." Die Zeit, 8 March, 1951.
64. TNA, PRO, FO 1056/276.
65. Ibid.
66. Bösch and Geppert, "Journalists as Political Actors".
67. Von Hodenberg, "Konsens und Krise", 460.
68. Hoffmann-Riem, "Rundfunk als Public Service".

References

Appelius, Stefan. *Heine: Die SPD und der lange Weg zur Macht* [Heine. The Social-Democratic Party and It's a Long Way into Power]. Essen: Klartext-Verlag, 1999.

Baade, Christina L. *Victory through Harmony. The BBC and Popular Music in World War II*. Oxford and New York: Oxford University Press, 2012.

Bayer, Karen. *"How dead is Hitler?" Der britische Starreporter Sefton Delmer und die Deutschen* [The British Star Reporter Sefton Delmer and the Germans]. Mainz: Philipp *von* Zabern, 2009.

BBC External Services, eds. *'Hier ist England' – 'Live aus London'. Das deutsche Programm der British Broadcasting Corporation 1938–1988* ['This is England' – 'Live from London'. The German-Language Programme by the BBC 1938–1988]. London: BBC External Services, 1988.

Biller, Marita. *Exilstationen: Eine empirische Untersuchung zur Emigration und Remigration deutschsprachiger Journalisten und Publizisten* [Stations of Exile. An Empirical Study on Emigration and Remigration of German Speaking Journalists and Publicists]. Münster: Lit Verlag, 1994.

Birke, Adolf M., Hans Booms, and Otto Merker. eds. *Akten der britischen Militärregierung in Deutschland: Sachinventar 1945–1955*. [Control Commission for Germany, British Element. Inventory 1945–1955]. 11 vols. München: Saur, 1993.

Bösch, Frank, and Dominik Geppert. "Journalists as Political Actors." In *Journalists as Political Actors: Transfers and Interactions between Britain and Germany Since the Late 19th Century*, edited by Frank Bösch and Dominik Geppert, 7–15. Augsburg: Wißner-Verlag, 2008.

Briggs, Asa. *The Birth of Broadcasting. Vol. I of The History of Broadcasting in the United Kingdom*. London: Oxford University Press, 1961.

Briggs, Asa. *The War of Words. Vol. III of The History of Broadcasting in the United Kingdom*. London: Oxford University Press, 1970.

Briggs, Asa. *Sound and Vision. Vol. IV of The History of Broadcasting in the United Kingdom*. London: Oxford University Press, 1979.

Brinson, Charmian, and Richard Dove, eds. *'Stimme der Wahrheit': German-Language Broadcasting by the BBC*. Amsterdam and New York: Rodopi, 2003.

Brüning, Jens. "Die BBC als Vorbild für den Nachkriegsrundfunk in Deutschland [The BBC as a Role Model for Broadcasting in Post-War Germany]." In *'Stimme der Wahrheit': German-*

Language Broadcasting by the BBC, edited by Charmian Brinson and Richard Dove, 93–116. Amsterdam and New York: Rodopi, 2003.

Chignell, Hugh. *The BBC Handbooks: Some Observations for Broadcasting Historians*. Accessed December 17, 2014. http://www.britishonlinearchives.co.uk/guides/9781851171385.php. Last updated: July 7th, 2008.

Clemens, Gabriele. *Britische Kulturpolitik in Deutschland 1945–1949. Literatur, Film, Musik und Theater* [British Cultural Politics in Germany 1945–1949. Literature, Music and Theatre]. Stuttgart: Steiner, 1997.

Clemens, Gabriele. "Remigranten in der Kultur- und Medienpolitik der Britischen Zone [Repatriated Germans in Cultural and Media Politics in the British Zone]." In *Zwischen den Stühlen? Remigranten und Remigration in der deutschen Medienöffentlichkeit* [To be Caught Between the Stools? Repatriated Germans and Repatriation in the German Public Sphere], edited by Claus-Dieter Krohn and Axel Schildt, 50–65. Hamburg: Hans Christians, 2002.

Đorđević, Mira. 2000. "Pioniere des deutschen Rundfunks im Spiegel eines Briefwechsels. Ernst Hardt – Alexander Maaß (1945/46) [Pioneers of German Broadcasting as Reflected in Correspondence. Ernst Hardt – Alexander Maaß]." Part I and II. *Rundfunk und Geschichte* 26, no. 1 (2000): 29–43; no. 2 (2000): 158–176.

Dove, Richard. "Introduction." In *'Stimme der Wahrheit': German-Language Broadcasting by the BBC*, edited by Charmian Brinson and Richard Dove, IX–XV. Amsterdam and New York: Rodopi, 2003.

Eberstadt, Walter Albert. *Whence We Came, Where We Went: From the Rhine to the Main to the Elbe, from the Thames to the Hudson. A Family History*. New York: W.A.E. Books, 2002.

Eumann, Marc Jan. *Der Deutsche Presse-Dienst. Nachrichtenagentur in der britischen Zone 1945–1949* [The German News Service. News Agency in the British Zone 1945–1949]. Köln: von Halem, 2011.

Goergen, Joachim. "Der britische Einfluß auf den deutschen Rundfunk 1945 bis 1948 [The British Influence on German Broadcasting 1945–1948]." PhD, Freie Universität, Berlin, 1983.

Greene, Hugh Carleton. "Anfänge des NWDR [The Beginnings of the NWDR]." In *Jahrbuch des Nordwestdeutschen Rundfunks* [Year Book of the NWDR]. 10–13. Hamburg: NWDR, 1950.

Greene, Hugh Carleton. *Entscheidung und Verantwortung: Perspektiven des Rundfunks* [Decision and Accountability: Perspectives of Broadcasting]. Hamburg: Hans-Bredow-Institut, 1970.

Harding, E. A. F. "The Past and Future of Staff Training." In *BBC Year Book 1947*, 29–33. London: The British Broadcasting Corporation, 1947.

Hilmes, Michele. *Network Nations. A Transnational History of British and American Broadcasting*. New York, NY: Routledge, 2012.

Hoffmann-Riem, Wolfgang. "Rundfunk als Public Service. Zur Vergangenheit, Gegenwart und Zukunft öffentlich-rechtlichen Rundfunks [Broadcasting as Public Service. On Past, Present and Future of Public Service Broadcasting]." *Medien und Kommunikationswissenschaft* 54, no. 1 (2006): 95–105.

Jacobmeyer, Wolfgang. "Politischer Kommentar und Rundfunkpolitik. Zur Geschichte des Nordwestdeutschen Rundfunks, 1945–1951 [Political Statement and Broadcasting Policy. On the History of the NWDR, 1945–1951]." *Vierteljahreshefte für Zeitgeschichte* 21, no. 4 (1973): 358–387.

REVISITING TRANSNATIONAL BROADCASTING

Krohn, Claus-Dieter, and Patrik von zur Mühlen, eds. *Rückkehr und Aufbau nach 1945. Deutsche Remigranten im öffentlichen Leben Nachkriegsdeutschlands* [Return and Reconstruction after 1945. Repatriated Germans in Post-war German Public Life]. Marburg: Metropolis-Verlag, 1997.

Kutsch, Arnulf. "Unter britischer Kontrolle: Der Zonensender 1945–1948 [Under British Control: The Broadcasting Station in the British Zone 1945–1948]." In *Der NDR: Zwischen Programm und Politik. Beiträge zu seiner Geschichte* [The NDR: Between Programme and Politics. Studies on Its History], edited by Wolfram Köhler, 83–148. Hannover: Schlüter, 1991.

Leighton-Langer, Peter. *X steht für unbekannt: Deutsche und Österreicher in den britischen Streitkräften im Zweiten Weltkrieg* [X Means Unknown. Germans and Austrians in British Forces during WW II]. Berlin: Berlin-Verlag Spitz, 1999.

Nicholas, Siân. *The Echo of War. Home Front Propaganda and the Wartime BBC, 1939–1945*. Manchester: Manchester University Press, 1996.

Pütter, Conrad. *Rundfunk gegen das 'Dritte Reich': Ein Handbuch* [Broadcasting Against the 'Third Reich'. A Handbook]. München: Saur, 1986.

Rasack, Bernhard. "Parteieneinfluß und Rundfunkaufsicht. Zur Entstehung des Bayerischen Rundfunkgesetzes [Party-political Influence and Supervision of Broadcasting. On the Introduction of a Law of Broadcasting in Bavaria]." *Rundfunk und Fernsehen* 22, no. 1 (1974), 53–67.

Reith, J. C. W. "Introduction." In *B.B.C. Hand Book*, 31–35. London: British Broadcasting Corporation, 1928.

Richter, Clas Oliver. *Political Warfare Executive*. Münster: Lit Verlag, 1998.

Roelle, Thomas. "Der britische Einfluß auf den Aufbau des Nordwestdeutschen Rundfunks [The British Influence on the Construction of the NWDR]." PhD, University of Kiel, 1990.

Ruge, Gerd. *Unterwegs: Politische Erinnerungen* [On the Road: Political Memoirs]. Berlin: Hanser, 2013.

Scannell, Paddy, and David Cardiff. "Public Service Broadcasting." In *1922–1939, Serving the Nation*. Vol. 1 *of A Social History of British Broadcasting*, edited by Paddy Scannell and David Cardiff, 3–19. Oxford: Basil Blackwell, 1991.

Schwarzkopf, Dietrich. *Ausbildung und Vertrauensbildung: Die Rundfunkschule des NWDR* [Training and Trust: The Training School of the NWDR]. Hamburg: Hans-Bredow-Institut, 2007. Accessed December 17, 2014. http://www.hans-bredow-institut.de/webfm_send/184.

Sozialdemokratische Partei Deutschlands, ed. *Denkschrift über Verfassung und Programmgestaltung des NWDR* [Memorandum on Constitution and Programme Planning of the NWDR]. Hannover: SPD, 1948.

Stuebs, Albin. "Was ist 'Rundfunkschule'? [What Is 'Training School'?]." In *NWDR-Jahrbuch 1950–1953*, 74–75. Hamburg, 1953.

Tracey, Michael. *Das unerreichbare Wunschbild. Ein Versuch über Hugh Greene und die Neugründung des Rundfunks in Westdeutschland nach 1945* [The Unreachable Ideal. An Attempt on Hugh Greene and the Reconstruction of Broadcasting in West Germany after 1945]. Köln: W. Kohlhammer, 1982.

Von Hodenberg, Christina. *Konsens und Krise: Eine Geschichte der westdeutschen Medienöffentlichkeit 1945–1973* [Consensus and Crisis. A History of the West German Media Public Sphere 1945–1973]. Göttingen: Wallstein Verlag, 2006.

Wagner, Hans-Ulrich. *Rückkehr in die Fremde? Remigranten und Rundfunk in Deutschland 1945 bis 1955* [Coming Home to a Foreign Country? Repatriated Germans and Broadcasting in Germany 1945–1955]. Berlin: Vistas, 2000.

Wagner, Hans-Ulrich. "Über alle Hindernisse hinweg: London-Remigranten in der westdeutschen Rundfunkgeschichte [Beyond All Obstacles. Repatriated Germans from London in West German Broadcasting History]." In *'Stimme der Wahrheit'. German-Language Broadcasting by the BBC*, edited by Charmian Brinson and Richard Dove, 139–157. Amsterdam and New York: Rodopi, 2003.

Wagner, Hans-Ulrich. "Das Ringen um einen neuen Rundfunk. Der NWDR unter der Kontrolle der britischen Besatzungsmacht [The Struggle for a New Broadcasting Station. The NWDR under Control of the Control Commission for Germany, British Element]." In *Die Geschichte des Nordwestdeutschen Rundfunks* [The History of the Northwest German Broadcaster], edited by Peter von Rüden and Hans-Ulrich Wagner, 13–84. Hamburg: Hoffmann und Campe, 2005.

Wagner, Hans-Ulrich. "'Wir müssen hart bleiben, wenn wir in Deutschland etwas Neues schaffen wollen.' Alexander Maaß an Ernst Hardt, November 1945 ['We Have to Stand Firm, If We Want to Build Up Something New in Germany.' Alexander Maaß to Ernst Hardt, November 1945]." In *Nach dem Krieg! – Nach dem Exil? Erste Briefe. First Letters. Fallbeispiele aus dem sozialwissenschaftlichen und philosophischen Exil* [After the War! – After the Exile? First Letters. Case Studies from the Social-scientific and the Philosophic Exile], edited by Detlef Garz and David Kettler, 177–187. München: edition text+kritik im Richard Boorberg Verlag, 2012.

Wallace, Ian. "'Lob der Emigration': Albin Stuebs ['Praise of Emigration': Albin Stuebs]." In *Fractured Biographies*, edited by Ian Wallace, 119–180. Amsterdam and New York: Rodopi, 2003.

THE BBC POLISH SERVICE DURING THE SECOND WORLD WAR

Agnieszka Morriss

During the Second World War the broadcasts of the BBC Polish Service became a major source of information in occupied Poland. Although listening to, or possessing, a radio was punishable by death under the German occupation, Poles were willing to risk their lives in order to hear the news from London. For many, the BBC remained the only contact with the outside world, whilst listening itself became a symbol of resistance. The Polish Service was required to follow the official line of British government's policy, presenting a positive picture of the USSR. Anything considered anti-Soviet was expunged. Given that the BBC European Service was designed as an instrument of British propaganda, the Polish Service was recognised as a powerful medium in territorial and political disputes between Poland and the USSR.

During the Second World War, the broadcasts of the BBC Polish Service became a major source of information in occupied Poland. Although listening to, or possessing, a radio was punishable by death under the German occupation, Poles were willing to risk their lives in order to hear the news from London. For many, the BBC remained the only contact with the outside world, whilst listening itself became a symbol of resistance. The broadcasts not only connected Poland with the rest of the world but also informed the Poles about what was happening in their own country. The BBC Polish Service played a significant role in transmitting news about the situation at the front as well as about internal political issues. Moreover, the BBC Polish Service co-operated with the Polish Underground Movement which monitored the British broadcasts and distributed clandestinely extracts in newspapers and leaflets. This cooperation, however, was not a direct one, but worked through the Polish government-in-exile, which in 1940 took refuge in London. The BBC Polish Service also exercised a significant influence by supporting Allied intelligence, sabotaging German actions and interrupting work in German factories. The broadcasts from London had an enormous impact on listeners in Poland since it established a link with the Polish government-in-exile whose representatives often spoke on the air, thus playing an important role in maintaining public morale. Since Britain was considered as Poland's most important ally, and given the fact that the news came from London, an illusion was created that Poland was the centre of the world's attention.[1]

My preliminary research reveals that the BBC Polish Service was required to follow the official line of the British government, presenting a positive picture of the USSR, Britain's ally from 1941 onwards. Anything considered anti-Soviet was expunged. Controversial issues such as the Polish-Soviet border, the deportation of Polish citizens, the arrests of

95

members of the Polish Home Army, or the Katyn massacre were labelled sensitive and withheld from the BBC broadcasts. As a result, the impartiality and credibility of the BBC were questioned in some quarters in Poland.

After the cessation of the diplomatic relations between Poland and the USSR in 1943, the subject of the post-war Polish-Soviet frontier became a major issue for the Polish government-in-exile. While the British government was willingly to act as a mediator between the Polish Prime Minister Mikolajczyk and Stalin, the BBC Polish Service was recognised as a powerful medium in the Polish-Soviet negotiations because of its wide audience in Poland and among the Polish Army fighting all over the world. Given that the BBC European Service was designed as an instrument of Britain's foreign policy, the BBC's Polish broadcasts represented a significant medium for convincing the Polish public to assent to the Soviet Union's territorial demands. Since the acceptance of the Curzon Line did not have the support of the Polish population, nor of the leaders of the Polish Underground, it was recognised that, rather than being grounded on logical argument, it would be necessary to 'sell' this policy to Poland by way or propaganda.[2] Further analysis points to the assumption that the British government, although aware of Soviet political manoeuvring, arrests and killings of the Polish Home Army, concealed information from the public and required that broadcasts to Poland should assume 'an increasingly emotional anti-German tone' and that 'the political questions should fall into the background' while not giving 'an impression that we are concealing anything'.[3] Similar treatment was given to the coverage of the Warsaw Rising in 1944 when the BBC Polish Service failed to inform Polish listeners comprehensively about the actual political and military situation. Although the Political Warfare Executive (PWE) already acknowledged in February 1944 that it was highly probable that the Red Army would occupy Poland, right until the end of the war the BBC Polish Service continued to suppress information which could in anyway undermine the Soviet Union's position as a friendly neighbouring country and guarantor of Poland's independence.

State of Research

An examination of the relevant literature demonstrates the limited nature of the work done to date on the BBC Polish Service during the Second World War. The importance of the Service in this period has been neglected by both English and Polish scholars. Asa Briggs (*The War of Words*), Gerard Mansell (*Let Truth to Be Told*) and Krzysztof Pszenicki (*Tu Mowi Londyn* [*This is London*]) are the only writers to have considered the BBC Polish Service within the historical framework of the BBC European Service.

Briggs contributes significantly, providing an in-depth analysis of the BBC European Service; its structure, organisation and internal relations, including the relationship between the PWE and the Foreign Office. However, little attention has been paid to the BBC Polish Service itself. The author discusses the listening conditions in Poland under German occupation and the role of the Polish Underground in monitoring the BBC's broadcasts as well as in distributing their content through the clandestine press. Moreover, he highlights the importance of the BBC Polish Service in sabotaging the German occupation forces in Poland. Briggs' main focus, however, is on Radio Polskie, the Polish-language programme organised by the Polish exile government (under close supervision of the British government) and transmitted by the BBC. In contrast, Mansell presents a more comprehensive account of the BBC Polish Service, drawing on interviews with former employees of the Service, including its editor, Gregory Macdonald. The book also offers a greater insight into the origins of the Service, its relations with the PWE and the Polish government-in-exile in London, and its internal affairs. Nevertheless, as is the case with Briggs, the Polish Service is only mentioned in the context of the overall structure and work of the BBC European Service; the analysis does not explore the actual content of the BBC's Polish broadcasts.

Pszenicki's *Tu Mowi Londyn* [*This is London*] is an excellent source of information about those who worked at the BBC Polish Service. However, it concentrates mainly on the post-war Communist era. The author relies heavily on the works of Briggs and Mansell and makes no references to primary sources. Moreover, discussion on wartime censorship is very limited. Also worth mentioning is Michael Fleming's *Auschwitz, the Allies and Censorship of the Holocaust*, which includes an analysis of the papers and bulletins of the BBC Polish Service. However, the main focus of this study is on the BBC's coverage and censorship of German atrocities committed in Auschwitz. In addition, valuable information on the impact of the BBC's Polish broadcasts on listeners in Poland can be found in Nowak's *Kurier z Warszawy* [*Courier from Warsaw*], Mazur's *Bureau of Information and Propaganda* [*Bureau of Information and Propaganda*] and in Kwiatkowski's *Polskie Radio w Konspiracji* [Polskie Radio in conspiracy].

Aims of Research

In addition to this literature, my thesis aims to provide a comprehensive account of the structure, organisation and output of the BBC Polish Service. Based on previously neglected archival sources, it will contribute to the histories of the BBC European Service, the BBC Monitoring Service, the PWE and the Polish government-in-exile, and it will expand our knowledge and understanding of the relationship and interaction between those institutions. Focusing on questions of wartime censorship and propaganda and on the coverage of issues which became a subject of dispute between the Polish and Soviet governments, the study analyses the extent to which the BBC Polish Service was used as an instrument of British foreign policy. Therefore, the principal research question is this: to what extent did the BBC Polish Service report objectively, representing, as was claimed during and after the war, the points of view of both the Polish and the Soviet governments? In order to answer this question, the analysis will focus on the level of compliance of the BBC Polish Service with the directives issued by the PWE and with the censorship guidelines of the Foreign Office. Special attention will also be paid to the BBC's relationship with the Polish government-in-exile, and in particular with the Polish Ministry of Information which also sought to influence the BBC's Polish-language output. In this context, we shall also examine the relationship and cooperation between the BBC Polish Service and Radio Polskie. Hence, the thesis will shed new light on the diplomatic relations between Poland, Britain and the USSR and on the spread of Communism in Eastern Europe during the Second World War.

Sources

The thesis draws on primary sources from the BBC Written Archives Centre in Caversham, notably scripts of the BBC Polish Service bulletins, minutes of meetings, propaganda

REVISITING TRANSNATIONAL BROADCASTING

and news directives, notes of correspondence, memoranda, European Intelligence Papers (e.g. Studies of European Audiences and output reports), BBC Monitoring Digests, and PWE directives for the BBC Polish Service. Moreover, it makes use of Foreign Office papers (National Archives, Kew, London) discussing the importance and difficulties of broadcasting to Poland. The Polish Underground Movement Study Trust and the Polish Institute and Sikorski Museum (both situated in London), among other important primary sources related to the Polish government-in-exile, its diplomatic relations with Britain and the USSR and on the exchange of information with the Polish Underground, hold documents on the relationship between the BBC Polish Service and the Polish Ministry of Information. Here, the main focus is on the Polish Ministry of Information, papers of Polish couriers and emissaries, and reports and correspondence from Radio Polskie employees who, in many cases, worked for both Radio Polskie and the BBC Polish Service. Wartime circumstances and repression during the Communist period in Poland resulted in the destruction of most of the documents. However, some of the scripts of the BBC'S Polish-language bulletins were monitored by the Polish Underground and can be found in the Central Archive of Modern Records in Warsaw. In addition, the thesis will make use, first, of material from the Hoover Institute at Stanford, notably memoranda and correspondence discussing the relationship between the Polish government-in-exile in London and the BBC Polish Service; second, of papers of the BBC Monitoring Service held at the Imperial War Museum archive at Duxford; and third, of Noel Newsome's collection of BBC European Service papers, private correspondence, memoranda, and the Studies of European Audience reports held at the Churchill Archives Centre at Churchill College Cambridge. The study also draws on a private collection of unpublished papers and articles of the wartime editor of the BBC Polish Service, Gregory MacDonald (currently in the possession of his son).

Disclosure Statement

No potential conflict of interest was reported by the author.

Notes

1. Nowak, Kurier z Warszawy.
2. Propaganda, Directives: Polish Service: PWE, 16 January 1944, BBC Written Archives Centre, Caversham, Reading, R34/663.
3. Political Warfare and Executive directives for Poland: broadcasts to Poland: Polish underground movement, 23 March 1944, The National Archives, London, FO 371/39422.

Bibliography

Bell, Philip M. H. *John Bull and the Bear: British Public Opinion, Foreign Policy and the Soviet Union: 1941–1945*. London: Hodder Arnold, 1990.
Briggs, Asa. *The War of Words. Vol . 3 of: The History of Broadcasting in the United Kingdom*. 2nd ed. Oxford: Oxford University Press, 1995.

Fleming, Michael. *Auschwitz, the Allies and Censorship of the Holocaust*. Cambridge: Cambridge University Press, 2014.

Garnett, David. *The Secret History of PWE: The Political Warfare Executive, 1939–1945*. London: St. Ermin's Press, 2002.

Halski, Czeslaw. *6 Lat: Perypetie Wojenne, 1939–1945* [6 Years: Wartime Peripeteia, 1939–1945]. London: Caldra House, 1991.

Kirkpatrick, Ivone. *The Inner Circle: Memoirs*. London: Macmillan, 1959.

Kwiatkowski, Maciej Jozef. *Polskie Radio w Konspiracji* [Polskie Radio in conspiracy: 1939–1946]. Warsaw: Panstwowy Instytut Wydawniczy, 1989.

Lean, Tangye E. *Voices in the Darkness: The Story of European Radio War*. London: Secker & Warburg, 1943.

Lockhart, Bruce R H. *Comes the Reckoning*. London: Arno Press, 1972.

Mansell, Gerard. *Let Truth Be Told: 50 Years of BBC External Broadcasting*. London: Weidenfeld and Nicolson, 1982.

Mazur, Grzegorz. *Biuro Informacji i Propagandy: SZP-ZWZ-AK, 1939–45* [Bureau of Information and Propaganda: SZP-ZWZ-AK, 1939–45]. Warsaw: Instytut Wydawniczy Pax, 1987.

Nowak, Jan. *Kurier z Warszawy* [Courier from Warsaw]. Warsaw: Odnowa, 2009.

Pszenicki, Krzysztof. *Tu Mowi Londyn: Historia Sekcji Polskiej BBC* [This is London: History of the Polish Section of the BBC]. Warsaw: Rosner & Wspólnicy, 2009.

Walker, Andrew. *A Skyful of Freedom: 60 Years of the BBC World Service*. London: Broadcast Books, 1992.

BROADCASTING BY THE CZECHOSLOVAK EXILE GOVERNMENT IN LONDON, 1939–1945

Erica Harrison

This project places the wartime BBC broadcasts of the Czechoslovak Government-in-exile at the centre of a study of their work in London, analysing their programmes as one aspect of their performance of authority. It is an AHRC-funded Collaborative Doctoral Award Project between the University of Bristol and Czech Radio in Prague, combining a close analysis of the broadcasts themselves with archival research into the Czechoslovak Government-in-exile and their relationship with the BBC. Like many Allied governments during the Second World War, the Czechoslovaks in London were permitted to broadcast to their people at home via the BBC European Service and these government programmes, distinct from the BBC's own Czech- and Slovak-language output, formed the only consistent connection between the exiles and the Czechoslovak public. The broadcasts were therefore vital to the establishment of the government's authority and right to lead, as well as being the means by which exile politicians communicated their policies and plans to listeners at home. Research into the exile government's relationship with the BBC confirms the overall success of their co-operation, but also highlights various points of tension in which the Corporation's priority of supplying occupied Europe with accurate news conflicted with the exile government's desire to pursue their own political agenda.

Analysis of the exile government programme and the negotiations behind it reveals a great deal not only about their policies and relations with their allies, but also about their understanding of the state they represented and its future position in the world. In the wartime context, when the Czechoslovak state had been destroyed and its return was not yet guaranteed, much of the exile government's broadcasting was dominated by a projection of their interpretation of Czechoslovak history and national identity. This research demonstrates that this interpretation relied strongly on the historical narrative popularised in the interwar period, on the memory of first Czechoslovak president Tomáš Garrigue Masaryk, and on the understanding of democracy as an inherently Czech characteristic as listeners were repeatedly told that, 'the Czech spirit is principally the ideal of freedom, the ideal of moral integrity, the ideal of humanity, of democracy'.[1] In their efforts to ensure the recreation of their state, the exile government strove to emphasise Czechoslovak unity in both a political and national sense but, as in the interwar republic, this resulted in a Czech-dominated Czechoslovak identity which left little room for discussion of Slovak issues. Broadcasters in London, both Czech and Slovak, struggled to agree on how best to address listeners in the nominally independent Slovak state, closely allied to Nazi Germany. Despite the complex questions of future Slovak representation being raised by Slovaks at home and in London, a combination of practical and ideological issues prevented the broadcasting of any concrete answers and the tone of the exile government's programme remained resolutely negative. Listeners were repeatedly told that the 'so-called independent Slovakia' was 'nothing but a toy in the hands of Adolf Hitler' and anyone saying otherwise was dismissed as 'either an idiot or a traitor'.[2]

A further issue facing the exile government in their radio work was that of broadcasting to Subcarpathian Ruthenia, a former Czechoslovak territory that had been occupied by Hungary in 1939. Even when they eventually overcame opposition from the Foreign Office in this matter, Czechoslovak broadcasters struggled with unresolved questions regarding the dominant language and identity of the region's population. The wartime broadcasts offer an interesting new source in the history of Subcarpathian Ruthenia as they constitute the final effort at communication between a Czechoslovak government and the people of a region that was to be incorporated into the Soviet Union in the immediate aftermath of the war. In addition to these national questions, the exile government programme also sought to keep listeners informed of the progress of the war, both in diplomatic and military terms, and the changing diplomatic relationships with allies such as Britain, Poland and—crucially—the Soviet Union are clearly reflected in the broadcasts. This study charts the impact that an increasingly close alliance with the USSR had on Czechoslovak political broadcasting, creating confused and conflicting messages in their programmes. In addition to increasing the prominence of the USSR in their programming and heaping praise on the military achievements of their Soviet ally, Czechoslovak exile government broadcasters also reverted to nineteenth-century arguments of ethnic ties among all 'brother Slavs' in their ongoing battle against Germany, their 'eternal enemy'.[3]

In this project, however, the wartime broadcasts are analysed not only as political texts but also as radio broadcasts, intended to be spoken aloud and heard by an audience in occupied Czechoslovakia who risked imprisonment and death by listening. While many recent theories on the nature of radio listening portray it as a background medium, generally listened to by an audience that is simultaneously engaged in another activity, the difficult conditions faced by those living under occupation demanded greater commitment to listening and brought the radio out of the background of daily life. This project also examines the techniques used by various prominent broadcasters, such as Foreign Minister Jan Masaryk, to establish a personal relationship with the audience. It analyses the capacity for radio to give an illusion of direct communication between speaker and listener and thereby create a sense of intimacy that can then be used to bolster support for government policy. Masaryk's characteristic humour and personable style of speech successfully exploited this characteristic of radio and made him the exile government's most popular speaker.

Sources

The original impetus for this project was the discovery of a collection of previously unstudied BBC wartime broadcasts, preserved at the Czech Ministry of Foreign Affairs since the end of the Second World War. Between 1948 and 1989 the communist regime in Czechoslovakia had impeded study of the London exile movement and the recordings had been inaccessible before their incorporation into this project. One year was spent in the archive at Czech Radio cataloguing these wartime broadcasts in order to make them available to the public and to programme-makers at Czech Radio itself. Further investigation into the recordings revealed them to be a combination of Czechoslovak broadcasts and programmes produced by the London Transcription Service, a branch of the BBC which sent both transcribed BBC broadcasts and its own original programming abroad for retransmission at subscribing radio stations. In addition to this new collection, the Czech Radio archive also holds the authorised texts of the Czechoslovak government programme and these form the principal primary source base for this project, supplemented by the published collections of broadcasts made by prominent Czechoslovak figures, such as President Edvard Beneš and Foreign Minister Masaryk.[4]

In addition to the texts of the programmes themselves, this project also uses broadcasting as a frame within which to analyse the Czechoslovak–British relationship. The collections held at the BBC Written Archives Centre in Caversham were used to build up an understanding of the Corporation's approach to allied exile governments but, unfortunately, the files relating directly to the BBC Czech Service in this period have been lost. Much still therefore remains unknown about the BBC Czech Service itself and the broadcasting it undertook without the co-operation of the exile government, although locating sources for further research in this area may prove difficult. BBC Intelligence Reports and Listener Surveys were also consulted to provide some information on how the government's broadcasts were received, but the occasional comments recorded there do not offer significant evidence for how the broadcasts were understood by the public at large and reception is the single largest field of future research suggested by this project. The information held at the Czech National Archive and the Czech Ministry of Foreign Affairs Archive regarding the exile government's work and the structure of their broadcasting was invaluable to this project, and the Foreign Office files held at the National Archives in Kew, London, shed light on the British side of the relationship. This project examines the exile government's broadcasts in the context of their British exile and highlights the points of contention between the two sides through their impact on the radio. The minutes of the exile government's meetings,[5] currently in the process of publication, are also a useful source for this project, and for future researchers studying the London exile movement.

State of Research

Prior to this project, study of the BBC's Czech Service had been minimal. As a small service representing a low-priority ally, the Czechoslovaks receive only passing references in British histories of the BBC and the only work dedicated solely to the BBC Czech Service is Milan Kocourek's *Volá Londýn* (London Calling, 2013),[6] a compilation of anecdotes and memories from former employees, focusing on the Cold War period. In terms of academic work, the structure of the service and the wartime broadcasts is covered in brief in histories of the Czech media but Jan Láníček demonstrated the potential value of the Czech Radio archive to future researchers in his case study on the representation of Jews in the BBC Czech broadcasts.[7] Much work remains to be done on the BBC Czech Service but, as the first extensive study of the Czechoslovak government's wartime broadcasts at the Corporation, this project seeks to contribute to the history of the BBC European Service overall, as well as offering new understandings of the Czechoslovak exile movement, the use of radio by political exiles, and the capacity for radio to further efforts at nation-building from a distance.

Disclosure Statement

No potential conflict of interest was reported by the author.

Notes

1. Czech Radio Archive, Prague, LN Z 1943–19, 26.3.43.
2. Ibid., LN Z 1940–2, 21.10.1940; LN Z 1941–4, 2.1.1941; Masaryk, *Volá Londýn,* 165.
3. Czech Radio Archive, Prague, LN Z 1941–7, 19.7.1941; LN Z 1941–33, 22.6.1944.
4. Beneš, *Šest let exilu a druhé světové války: Řeči, projevy a dokumenty z r.* 1938–1945, 1945.
5. Němeček, *Zápisy ze schůzí československé vlády.*
6. Kocourek, *Volá Londýn,* 2013.
7. Láníček, *The Czechoslovak Service of the BBC,* 2010.

References

BBC *Londýn Zpravodajství [LN Z].* Czech Radio Archive.

BBC "Wartime Broadcast Collection [Working title]." Czech Radio Archive.

Beneš, Edvard. *Šest let exilu a druhé světové války: Řeči, projevy a dokumenty z r. 1938–1945* [Six Years of Exile and the Second World War: Speeches, Addresses and Documents From 1938–1945]. London: Týdeník Čechoslovák, 1945.

Kocourek, Milan. *Volá Londýn: Historie českého a slovenského vysílání BBC* [London Calling: The History of Czech and Slovak Broadcasting by the BBC]. Prague: Ottovo nakladatelství, 2013.

Láníček, Jan. "The Czechoslovak Service of the BBC and the Jews During World War II." *Yed Vashem Studies* 38, no. 2 (2010): 123–153.

Masaryk, Jan. *Volá Londýn* [London Calling]. Prague: Panorama, 1990.

Němeček, Jan, Ivan, Šťovíček, Helena, Jan, Nováčková, Jan Kuklík, Jan, Bílek. eds. *Zápisy ze schůzí československé vlády v Londýně* [Minutes from Meetings of the Czechoslovak Government in London]. 3 vols. Prague: Historický ústav Akademie věd ČR, Masarykův ústav a Archiv Akademie věd ČR, 2008–2012.

Index

Adenauer, Konrad 85–7
Africa 3, 49–50, 69–70, 72
Alba, Duke of (Stuart, Jacobo
    Fitz-James) 50
Albania 6
Allies: bombing of France 70–1, 73; Dieppe,
    France, landing at 72–3; military
    failures, effect of 72–3; North Africa,
    landing in 72; Norway 16, 22–6; Sicily,
    landing in 56–7
Anglophilia 68, 71
anti-British propaganda 62–3, 66–73
appeasement policy 6, 16–18, 19, 25–6,
    49–50, 55–8
Arabic Service (BBC) 5–6, 49
Asian populations 4
Atkinson, William 52
Atlantic Charter 57
Auschwitz 97
Austria, annexation of 49
authoritarian governments 5, 7, 34, 45, 50
Axis 3, 5, 33–5, 38–9, 41, 44, 50, 57
Azores Agreement 41–4

Baldwin, Stanley 49
Balkans 6
Barea, Arturo 54
Barea, Elsa 54
Battle of Britain 66
BBC Arabic Service 5–6, 49
BBC Czech Service 102
BBC Danish Service 6
BBC Empire Service 3–4, 35

BBC European Services: BBC Polish Service
    96–7; Czechoslovak exile government
    in London 100; foreign policy 96;
    grant-in-aid 4; inauguration 4; political
    supervision 52
BBC External Services 4
BBC foreign language services 4–6: Axis
    5; BBC World Service, renaming as
    4; Eastern Europe 6; expansion 4;
    Latin America, German influence
    in 49; news bulletins 5; number of
    languages 4; objectivity 4–5; Overseas
    Broadcasting Service 50; propaganda
    3, 4–5; Radio London 49; resistance,
    stirring up popular 5; South America 49;
    Supervisor 18
BBC French Service 5, 62–73; Allied
    bombing of France 70–1, 73;
    Allied military failures, effect of
    72–3; Anglophilia 68, 71; anti-British
    propaganda 62–3, 66–73; arguments
    and counter-arguments from 1941
    68–73; Armistice with Germany 62,
    64, 67; censorship 64–5; *Chronique
    d'Angleterre* 69; conscience clause 65;
    Courrier de France 68–9, 73; directives
    65–6; Director of Propaganda
    Services 70; Egypt, attacks on 69;
    establishment of BBC French Service 7,
    63; expansionism of France 69–70; Free
    France 62–3, 67–9, 72–3; French Empire
    69–70; French nationals 68; 'French
    speak to the French' programme 7,

INDEX

63–4; *Ici la France* programme 64;
letters 67–9, 73; message repetition
68; news bulletins 64, 69; North Africa
70, 72; Political Warfare Executive
(PWE) 65–6, 69, 73; post-war France,
issue of 65, 72–3; provision, policy and
practice 64–6; public opinion 67–8, 70;
Radio Paris 63, 68–9; Radio Vichy 63,
66–9; *Radiodiffusion nationale (RN)* 64;
representations of Britain to occupied
France 5, 62–73; resistance 62–3, 68,
71; sovereignty of France 65, 72–3;
translations 64; Vichy France 63–73;
voices of freedom 63
BBC German Service 6, 14–26;
appeasement policy 6, 16–18, 19, 25–6;
BBC Foreign Languages Supervisor
18; British Embassy 20; censorship
22; Chamberlain's propaganda
campaign 1938–1940 6, 14–26;
committee of ministers, creation of
18; credibility 6, 16, 23–5; democracy
over totalitarianism, superiority of
19, 22; Department of Propaganda
in Enemy Countries (Department
EH) 18, 21–5; Foreign Office 14,
17–22, 24–5; government intervention
14–18, 20–2; leaflets 17, 20; military
preparedness, lack of 17; Ministry of
Information 16; National Council of
Labour 20; national interest 16, 20, 25;
Norway, Allied campaign in 16, 22–6;
objectivity 6, 14–16, 19, 22, 25; origins
of BBC German Service 16; political
commentaries and talks 18, 19–20;
Political Warfare Executive (PWE) 16;
pre-war propaganda strategy between
1938–1939 18–20; propaganda
strategy, evolution of 6, 16–26; public
opinion, influencing 6, 23–4; resistance,
stirring up popular 17, 21, 24; Service
Departments 21–3; straight news or
propaganda 18–20, 22; totalitarianism
15–19; truth 6, 14–16, 19, 22–5; wartime
propaganda strategy 20–8 *see also*

public service broadcasting to northern
post-war Germany (1945–1950),
transfer of
BBC Home Service 4
BBC Italian Service 6
BBC Monitoring Service 97–8
BBC Overseas Service 4
BBC Polish Service: anti-Soviet content
95–6; BBC European Service 96–7; BBC
Monitoring Service 97–8; censorship
97; communism 97–8; employees
95–8; Foreign Office papers 98; frontier
with Soviet Union, issue of 95–6;
government-in-exile 95–8; impartiality
96; Polish Underground Movement
95–6, 98; Political Warfare Executive
(PWE) 96–8; political issues 95–6; Radio
Polskie 96–8; resistance 95; Second
World War, during 95–8; sources of
information 97–8; Soviet Union 7, 95–7;
This is London programme 97
BBC Portuguese Service 6–7, 33–45;
Armando Cortesão crises 37–8;
authoritarian governments 7, 34,
45; Axis dictatorships, links with
33–5, 38–9, 41, 44; Azores Agreement
41–4; BBC Empire Service 35; British
Embassy 33, 36, 40, 44; censorship
33; colonies 38–9, 41–4; communism
37–9, 41, 44; Communist Party and
anarchists, contact with 39; creation
of BBC Portuguese Service 34–6;
credibility 34; criticism of regime, lack
of 35–7; D-Day 43; democracy 36–7,
40–5; editorial lines 7, 35, 39–43;
Estado Novo (New State) 33–44; exiles
35, 37–8, 42–4; flattery 35–6, 38–9,
44–5; Foreign Office 33–6, 38–41,
44–5; German propaganda campaign
7, 33–6, 39–40; guidelines 37–9;
increase in audience 16; instability or
disturbances 36–7, 41; interference
in internal affairs of Portugal 36–8,
41, 43–5; internal opposition 39, 45;
Ministry of Information 38, 41–2, 44;

INDEX

Monday Chronicle series 42–3; network of contacts, establishment of 39–41; neutrality in WWII 33–4, 39, 42–4; news bulletins 33, 38; number of listeners 34; objectives of service 38; objectivity 16, 34, 44; Portuguese Embassy in London 37; posters and brochures by Germany 33; public opinion 33; raw materials to Nazi Germany, British policy to end exports of 7, 41–5; Salazar, relations with 35–45; Second World War, during 6–7, 33–45; 'the Shell Network' 39–41; soft diplomacy 35; Soviet Union 37–8, 41, 44; Spain 34, 35, 44; Special Operation Executive (SOE) 39–40; Surveillance and State Defence Police (PVDE) 39–40; talks 35–44; truth 34; tungsten to Germany, export of 7, 41–5

BBC Radio Bari 3

BBC Spanish Service 48–58; appeasement, policy of 49–50, 55–8; bribery 51; British Embassy 7, 51, 54–8; Civil War 6, 49–50, 53; *Comentarios Londinenses* 53; complacent detachment, policy of 57; consolidation 48; controversies 53–4; counter-attack, onset of radio 51–3; culture 53; democracy 57–8; economic agreement with UK 51–2; economic aid 51–2; editorial approach 56–8; exile 50, 52, 54; Falangist Press 51; Foreign Office 49–53, 55–8; foreign policy 48, 57; German presence in Spain 49, 51; German propaganda 7, 49–55; Gibraltar 50–1; instability or disturbances in Portugal, reports of 36–7; internal affairs of Spain, interference with 49, 56–7; internal resistance 51, 57; launch of service 48, 50–1; Ministry of Information 50–2, 54–6; Morocco 50; neutrality 51, 53, 57; news bulletins 52; newsletters 51; Political Warfare Executive (PWE) 56; Portugal, reports of instability or disturbances in 36–7; pro-Nazi position of Franco's government 48, 51, 56–7; reception, interference

with 54; recognition of Franco's regime 50, 58; Second World War 6–7, 48–58; Spanish ambassador in London 50; talks 52–3, 56–7; United Nations, condemnation of Franco regime by 58; *La Voz de Londres* 52–3, 56–7; War Cabinet 48; wolfram exports to Axis 50, 57

BBC World Service 4–5

Beevor, Jack 40

Beigbeder, Juan 50–1, 52

Beneš, Edvard 102

Bennett, Jeremy 6

Bishop, WH Alexander 81

'black' radio stations 82

Blitzkrieg 24

bombing of France 70–1, 73

Boulogne-Billancourt, France, RAF bombing of Renault factory in 70–1

Bourdan, Pierre 62, 65, 71

Bracken, Brendan 49, 54

Brazil 38

Bredow, Hans 84

Brenan, Gerald 53

bribery 51

Briggs, Asa 5, 96–7

Brinson, Charmian 80

British Broadcasting Council, repositioning as BBC of 79

British Council 50

British Embassy: BBC German Service 20; BBC Portuguese Service 33, 36, 40, 44; BBC Spanish Service 7, 51, 54–8

British spirit 66, 83, 87–8

Brooks, Tim 63, 65

Brüggemann, Michael 2

Brunius, Jacques 62

Bulgaria 6

Burns, Tom 48, 51, 55–6

Buylla, Vicente 52

Cadogan, Alexander 18–19, 50, 55

Campbell, Ronald 36–7, 40

Canaris, Wilhelm 52

Cardiff, David 15, 16

INDEX

Carnation Revolution of 1974, Portugal 45

Castillejo, José 43, 52

censorship 22, 33, 64–5, 97

Chadwick, Kay 63

Chamberlain, Neville 6, 14–26, 35, 49, 51, 64

Cheke, Marcus 36

Christian Democratic Union (CDU) 84, 86–7

Churchill, Winston 24, 42, 48, 51, 56–8, 64, 73

Clark, RT 49

Cold War 1, 5

Cologne radio station 81–2

colonies 3, 38–9, 41, 44, 69–70

communism 37–9, 41, 44, 86–7, 97–8, 101

conflicts of interest 6

Control Commission for Germany/British
Element (CCG/BE) 80–1, 83–4

Cooper, Duff 49, 51, 54

Cortesão, Armando 35, 37–8

Cossío, Natalia 52

credibility 6, 16, 23–5, 34

Crémieux-Brilhac, Jean-Louis 63

Creyssel, Paul 63, 70–2

culture 5, 53

Curie, Eve 67

Curran, James 15–16

Curzon Line 96

Czechoslovak exile government in
London 1939-1945, broadcasting by
the 7, 100–2; BBC Czech Service 102;
communism 101; democracy 100;
diplomatic relationships 101; ethnic ties
101; exiles 100–2; Foreign Office 101–2;
government-in-exile 100–2; languages
100–1; London Calling programme
102; London Transcription Service
102; national identity 100–1; political
agenda 100–1; sources of information
101–2; Soviet Union 7, 101

D-Day 43, 57

Daily Worker 38

Daladier, Edouard 49

Dalton, Hugh 49

Danish Service (BBC) 6

Darlan, François, assassination of 72

Darlon, François 69

de Gaulle, Charles 62–4, 72

Delmer, Sefton 80

democracy 4–5; BBC German Service 7,
19, 22, 80, 83, 86–7; BBC Portuguese
Service 36–7, 40–5; BBC Spanish Service
57–8; Czechoslovak exile government
in London 100

demilitarisation 80

Deutscher Freiheitssender 29,8 82

Diego Suarez, Madagascar 70

Dieppe, France, Allied landing at 72–3

Dimbleby, Richard 49

diplomatic practices: BBC Portuguese
Service 35; cultural diplomacy 5;
Czechoslovak exile government
in London 101; new diplomacy 1;
propaganda 6; public diplomacy 2–3;
secrecy 1; soft diplomacy 35

Dove, Richard 80

Dovifat, Emil 87

Duchesne, Jacques 64–5, 72

Dunkirk, retreat at 66–7

Eberstadt, Walter Albert 81

Eck, Hélène 63

economic aid 51–2

The Economist 20

Eden, Anthony 49, 54, 56–7, 72–3

editorial lines 7, 35, 39–43, 56–8

Egerton, F Clement C 37

Egypt 69

elections 83–4

Ellul, Jacques 65

embassies: BBC Portuguese Service 37;
BBC Spanish Service 7, 50 see also
British Embassy

Empire Service (BBC) 3, 4, 35

employees: BBC Polish Service 95–8;
BBC Portuguese Service 35, 37–8,
42–4; BBC Spanish Service 50, 52,
54; Czechoslovak exile government
in London 100–2; public service
broadcasting to northern post-war
Germany, transfer of 7, 80–6

INDEX

Epton, Nina 69
ethnic ties 101
European Service *see* BBC European
 Services
Everitt, Walter 81
exiles: BBC Polish Service 95–8; BBC
 Portuguese Service 35, 37–8, 42–4;
 BBC Spanish Service 50, 52, 54;
 Czechoslovak exile government in
 London 100–2; governments-in-
 exile 95–8, 100–2; public service
 broadcasting to northern post-war
 Germany, transfer of 7, 80–7
External Services (BBC) 4

Fabian Society 54
First World War 2
Flanders, Allen 84
Fleming, Michael 87
foreign language services *see* BBC foreign
 language services
Foreign Office (FO) 5; BBC European
 Service 4; BBC German Service 14,
 17–22, 24–5; BBC Polish Service 98;
 BBC Portuguese Service 33–6, 38–41,
 44–5; BBC Spanish Service 49–53, 55–8;
 Czechoslovak exile government in
 London 101–2; Spanish Civil War 49
foreign policy: BBC European Services 96;
 BBC German Service 16; BBC Spanish
 Service 48, 57; Czechoslovak exile
 government in London 7
France: fall of France 24 *see also* BBC
 French Service
Franco, Francisco 3, 7, 34–5, 49–58
Fraser, Lindley 21
Fraud, Alberto Jiménez 53
Free France 62–3, 67–9, 72–3
freedom of speech 19, 22, 33

Garnett, David 5
Garrigue, Tomáš 100
General Strike 1926 15
Germany *see* BBC German Service; public
 service broadcasting to northern

post-war Germany (1945–1950),
 transfer
Giblin, Helen 5
Gibraltar 50–1
Gillie, Darsie 64–5
Goebbels, Joseph 80
Graves, Cecil 50
Greece 6
Greene, Hugh Carleton 82–6
Grimme, Adolf 86
Grisewood, Harman 44, 52, 57
Gullion, Edward 2

Halifax, Viscount (Wood, Edward) 18
Hamburg radio station 81–2
Hansestadt Hamburg, West Germany 84
Hardt, Ernst 82
Hayes, Carlton H 57
Heine, Fritz 84–5, 87
Henriot, Philippe 63, 65, 70–3
Hitler, Adolf 16–17, 19–21, 23–4, 36, 48–9,
 51–2, 54, 58, 67, 101
Hoare, Samuel 7, 48, 51–2, 54–8
Hodgeson, Robert 52
Hoffmann-Riem, Wolfgang 88
Home Service (BBC) 4
Hull, Cordell 42

ideals of public service 79–80, 83, 88
impartiality 19, 35, 96
independent and investigative journalism 83
instability or disturbances 36–7, 41
interference in internal affairs 36–8, 41,
 43–5, 49, 56–7
Islamic State (ISIS) 1
Italy 3, 6, 7, 49, 56–7

Japan 70
Jennings, Eric 63
Jowett, Garth S 2

Katyn massacre 96
Kirkpatrick, Ivone 50, 52, 54–6
Kocourek, Milan 102
Kwiatkowski, Maciej Jozef 97

INDEX

Láníček, Jan 102
Latin America 3, 38, 49
Lebanon 69
Leeper, Rex 14, 19, 50
Lefèvre, Pierre 62
Leigh Ashton, Anthony 51
licence fee 79
The Listener 14
LoBiundo, Ester, 6
Luneau, Aurélie 63

Maaß, Alexander 81–3, 86–7
McCann, William 52, 56
Macdonald, Gregory 97–8
Macmillan, Hugh (Lord Macmillan) 44
Madagascar 70
Malley, Bernard 51
The Manchester Guardian 14
Mansell, Gerard 5, 24–5, 96–7
Marks, John 52, 54
Martelli, Charles 35
Martínez Nadal, Rafael 48, 52–3, 55–8
Marzano, Arturo 6
Masaryk, Jan 101–2
Mazur, Grzegorz 97
Miall, Leonard 18
Middle East 49
Mikołajczyk, Stanisław 96
military failures, effect of Allied 72–3
Monitoring Service (BBC) 97–8
Monteiro, Armindo 37
Morocco 50
Munich crisis 1938 3, 16–17, 49, 79
Mussolini, Benito 49, 57
myth of the BBC 79

national identity 100–1
neutral countries 5; Portugal 33–4, 39,
    42–3; Spain 34, 44, 49, 51, 53, 57; UK
    neutrality in Spanish Civil War 49
New European Order 24
news bulletins 5, 33, 38, 49, 52, 64, 69, 80
Newsome, Noel 22–3, 50, 54, 98
Niedersachen, West Germany 84
Nordrhein-Westfalen, West Germany 84

Nordwestdeutscher Rundfunk (NWDR)
    80–7
North Africa 3, 49–50, 69–70, 72
northern Germany *see* public service
    broadcasting to northern post-war
    Germany (1945–1950), transfer of
Norway 16, 22–6
Nowak, Jan 97
Nye, Joseph 2

Oberlé, Jean 62–3, 67–8, 72
objectivity: BBC foreign language services
    4–5; BBC German Service 6, 14–16, 19,
    22, 25; BBC Portuguese Service 16, 34,
    44; propaganda 4–5, 6
O'Donnell, Victoria 2
Ogilvie, Frederick 49–50, 51–2
Onaindía, Alberto 52–3
Overseas Service (BBC) 4, 50

Palestine 3
Partner, Peter 5–6
Passera, Françoise 63
Pedro, António 42–4
Peers, Alison 52
Péri, Gabriel 71
Pessis, Jacques 63
Pétain, Philippe 66–7, 69–70
Philippe, Prince, Duke of Orléans 52
phoney war 20–1, 22, 25, 64
Poland *see* BBC Polish Service
Political Warfare Executive (PWE) 56, 65–6,
    69, 73, 79–80, 96–8
politics: BBC European Services 52; BBC
    German Service 16, 18, 19–20; BBC
    Polish Service 95–6; Czechoslovak
    exile government in London 100–1;
    public service broadcasting to
    northern post-war Germany, transfer
    of 83–8
Portugal 3, 39–40, 49 *see also* BBC
    Portuguese Service
post-war Germany *see* public service
    broadcasting to northern post-war
    Germany (1945–1950), transfer

INDEX

propaganda: Anglo-Italian propaganda 6; anti-British propaganda 62–3, 66–73; BBC foreign language services 3, 4–5; BBC French Service 62–3, 66–73; BBC German Service 6, 14–26; BBC Portuguese Service 7, 33–6, 39–40; BBC Spanish Service 7, 49–55; definition 2, 3; democracy over totalitarianism, superiority of 4–5; diplomacy 6; First World War 2; objectivity 4–5, 6; pejorative connotations 2, 3, 15; public opinion, influencing 1–2, 15; truth 6, 15

Pszenicki, Krzysztof 96–7

public opinion: BBC French Service 67–8, 70; BBC German Service 6, 23–4; BBC Portuguese Service 33; cultivation of public opinion 1–2; propaganda 1–2, 15; Spanish Civil War, UK public opinion on 49

Public Relations/Information Services Control Group (PR/ISC) 81

public service broadcasting to northern post-war Germany (1945–1950), transfer of 79–88; British Occupation Zone 80–4; British spirit 83, 87–8; Broadcasting Board (Rundfunkrat) 88; Broadcasting Control Unit (BCU) 81; Broadcasting school 82–3; checks and balances 85; Christian Democratic Union (CDU) 84, 86–7; Cologne station 81–2; communism 86–7; conservative press 86–7; Control Commission for Germany/British Element (CCG/BE) 80–1, 83–4; democratisation 7, 80, 83, 86–7; demilitarisation 80; Educational Interests 85; elections 83–4; exile, Germans in 7, 80–7; 'future of the Broadcasting in the British Zone' 84; German employees 7, 80–6; German News Service 80; Hamburg station 81–2; Hauptausschuss (Principal Committee) 85, 88; independent and investigative journalism 83; Information Control Units 81; intermediaries 80; Nordwestdeutscher Rundfunk (NWDR)

80–7; NWDR Außenreferat (Department of Foreign Affairs) 85; NWDR-Statut 84–6; personnel policies 84, 86; Political Division of CCG/BE 83–4; Political Forum programme 85–6; political influences 82, 85–7; political parties 83–8; political resistance to public service broadcasting 83–4; Political Warfare Executive (PWE) 79–80; practical tests for NWDR in 1948/1949 86–7; Public Relations/Information Services Control Group (PR/ISC) 81; public service ideals 79–80, 83, 88; recruiting new personnel 7, 80–2; refusal and rejection, concepts of 80; repatriated Germans, role of 7, 80–2; Resettlement school 82; Rundfunkbeirat des Kulturpolitischen Ausschusses (Broadcasting Advisory Board of the Committee for Cultural Policy) 84–5; Secretarial school 82–3; Social Democratic Party (SDP) 84–7; Training School (NWDR) 82–3, 86–7; truth 80; United States 80–1, 84; Verwaltungsrat (Administration Board) 85; Weimar Republic 80, 82; Zonal Advisory Council 84–5

Radio Bari 3
Radio London 49
Radio Paris 63, 68–9
Radio Polskie 96–8
Radio Vichy 63, 66–9
RAF (Royal Air Force) 65–6, 70–1, 73
Raskop, Heinrich Georg 86–7
raw materials to Germany, export of 7, 41–5, 50, 57
Reeves, Cecilia 64–5, 67, 69
refugees 49
Reith, John 15, 79
Renault factory in Boulogne-Billancourt, France, RAF bombing of 70–1
resistance movements: BBC Danish Service 6; BBC foreign language services 5; BBC French Service 62–3, 68, 71; BBC German Service 17, 21, 24; BBC Polish

INDEX

Service 95; BBC Portuguese Service 36–9, 41, 43–5; BBC Spanish Service 51, 57

Reuters 50

Ribeiro, Nelson 6, 16

Roberts, Frank 56

Romania 6

Roosevelt, FD 56–7

Royal Air Force (RAF) 65–6, 70–1, 73

Royal Charter of BBC 79

Ruge, Gerd 83

Saint-Denis, Michael 64

Saint-Nazaire, France, RAF bombing of 71

Salazar, António de Oliveira 7, 33–45

Sargent, Orme 19, 22

Scannell, Paddy 15, 16

Schleswig-Holstein, West Germany 84

Schultz, Walter D 85–7

Schumacher, Kurt 87

Schumann, Maurice 66–7, 71

Seaton, Jean 15–16

Selby, Walford 33–4

Serrano Súñer, Ramón 52–3, 55

'the Shell Network' 39–41

Sicily, Allied Landing in 56–7

Smuts, Jan 72–3

Snow, Nancy 2

Social Democratic Party (SDP) 84–7

soft power 2

South America 49

Soviet Union: BBC Polish Service 7, 95–7; BBC Portuguese Service 37–8, 41, 44; Czechoslovak exile government in London 7, 101; Germany, invasion by 38; Poland, frontier with 95–7; Radio Moscow 3; Spanish volunteer unit 57

Spain: neutrality 34, 44; Portugal 34, 35, 44, 39–40; Spanish Republican Radio 82 *see also* BBC Spanish Service; Spanish Civil War

Spanish Civil War: BBC Portuguese Service 35; BBC Spanish Service 49–50, 53; Broadcasting Control Unit (BCU) 82; Foreign Office 48; German participation

49; Italian stations 3; neutrality of UK 49; news bulletins 49; Portuguese stations 3; public opinion in UK 49; refugees 49

Spanish to South America, broadcasts in 49

Special Operation Executive (SOE) 39–40

Stalin, Josef 96

Stefanidis, Ioannis 6

Stenton, Michael 5, 63

'Stimme der Wahrheit': German-Language Broadcasting by the BBC. Brinson, Charmian and Dove, Richard 80

Strang, William 36

Stuart, Jacobo Fitz-James (Duke of Alba) 50

Stuebs, Albin 86–7

Subcarpathian Ruthenia 101

Sudetenland 16

Syria, German use of airbases in 69

The Tablet 52

talks 18–19, 35–44, 52–3, 56–7, 84–6

Tallents, Stephen 50

Tangiers, Tunisia 51, 56

Taylor, Philip M 2, 4, 5

The Times 14

Tognarini, Niccolò 6

Tomer, Eduardo Martínez 52

totalitarianism 4–5, 15–19, 22, 80

transborder media: definition 2; global media 2; government policy 5; importance 1; international media 2; national media with a transnational mission 2; pan-regional media 2; types 2

Trotter, William 53

truth: BBC German Service 6, 14–16, 19, 22–5, 80; BBC Portuguese Service 34; propaganda 6, 15

tungsten to Germany, export of 7, 41–5

United Nations (UN) 41, 44, 58

United States: BBC Portuguese Service 38; BBC Spanish Service 56; public service

INDEX

broadcasting to northern post-war Germany, transfer of 80–1, 84
USSR *see* Soviet Union

Vaillant, Derek 64
The Voice of Spain 50
Voigt, Frederick A 22
von Hodenberg, Christina 88
von Stohrer, Eberhard 54
von Zahn, Peter 81, 86

Warsaw Uprising 96
Weimar Republic 80, 82
Williams, Michael 57
wolfram exports to Axis 50, 57
Wood, Edward (Viscount Halifax) 18
Woodruff, Douglas 52
World Service (BBC) 4–5

Yencken, Arthur 54
Yugoslavia 6